# BUILDING
# WINDOWS
# INTO MEN'S
# SOULS

Brian Boughton

Brian Boughton's right to be identified as the author of this work has
been asserted by him in accordance with the Copyright,
Designs and Patents Act 1988.
All rights reserved.
No part of this book may be reproduced by any means electronic or
mechanical, including photocopy or any information storage or retrieval
system without permission in writing from the publisher.
A CIP catalogue record of this book is available from the British Library
Published, printed and bound by Amazon Kindle
ISBN 978-0-9540019-9-5

# DISCLAIMER

The descriptions of the church visits are the author's and the historical accounts are all taken from public domain.

The author has done his best to confirm them and if they contain inaccuracies he will correct them.

Most can be checked in a public library or on the Internet.

The illustrations are from Wikimedia Commons.

*To Elizabeth*

# CONTENTS

Introduction ................................................................. 1

1. Church Of England ................................................. 4

2. The Roman Catholics ............................................ 12

3. The Methodists .................................................... 21

4. The Pentecostal Church ........................................ 25

5. The Baptist Church .............................................. 30

6. The Spiritualist Church ......................................... 34

7. The Scientologists ............................................... 40

8. The Unitarians .................................................... 47

9. Jehovah's Witnesses ............................................. 51

10. The Jews .......................................................... 65

11. The Mormons ..................................................... 77

12. The Bahá'ís ...................................................... 86

13. The Quakers ...................................................... 94

14. The Salvation Army ........................................... 102

15. The Bruderhof .................................................. 112

16. Sunday Assembly ............................................... 115

The Author .......................................................... 118

# Introduction

I was christened in the Church of England and went to Sunday school to learn the Bible stories, following which I was confirmed as a teenager and served at Holy Communion.

But then I went to university and became a non-believer, remaining an atheist until old age. Some Bible scholars make a strong case that Jesus Christ may never have existed and the Gospels are a religious myth. So, on Sunday mornings when the church bells rang across the town, I went for walks in the countryside, to enjoy the flowers and listen to the birds.

In contrast, my wife was a devout Christian who went to church every Sunday and served three vicars on the Parochial Church Council. When she fell seriously ill, she asked me to look again at Christianity, which I promised I would. After she died, I went to all the local churches to learn about their different customs and beliefs.

And what an experience it turned out to be. The various denominations have many similarities such as praying, Bible reading and hymn singing, but they have differences that are interesting and sometimes fundamental.

The Anglican Church of England is the established Church which serves the Crown and Parliament. The monarch is its supreme head, and its archbishop is appointed by the Prime Minister and crowns the king at his coronation.

Methodists are similar to the Anglicans but reject the supremacy of the monarch and the authority of bishops.

Pentecostals emphasise the Holy Spirit which descended upon the apostles with tongues of fire, and they also practise faith healing.

Baptists stress the baptism of sentient adults and believe that non-baptised children can still go to heaven if they die.

Quakers prefer silent worship and reflection, and Spiritualist Church clairvoyants communicate with the dead and pass messages from them to their living relatives.

The Church of Scientology claims a unique origin of mankind and a scientific basis for their relationship with God.

The Jehovah's Witnesses emphasise Bible study and doorstep evangelism, while the Salvation Army administers care for the poor and destitute, and those who have fallen on misfortune.

The Mormons have given up their original belief in polygamy, but still value the importance of family life, and help with searches of family ancestry.

And Bahá'ís gather together for worship with other faiths,

both Christians and non-Christians.

Over and above all of these, the Roman Catholic church is the old, original church, which was founded by St Peter as the rock on which Christ could build his kingdom. It is by far the largest church and is ruled across the world by an infallible pope in Rome.

Few of us in England now go to church, but most of us wonder where we came from, who we are and where we're going when we die. Or as Paul Gaugin once said, 'D'où venons-nous? Qui sommes-nous? Où allons-nous?'

I will always be grateful to my wife for sending me on this odyssey, and I hope my experiences will interest church goers and others alike, and especially children setting out in life and studying religion at school. There are many different Christian faiths, and all of them give us pause for thought.

# 1. Church Of England

*The Archbishop of Canterbury*

I was born an Anglican and my parish church is only a short walk from where I live. So, it seemed reasonable to start with the Anglicans. But when I visited, at Holy Communion there were just 20 in the congregation from a parish of 5000 and all of them were elderly.

Some years ago, my parish had appointed a woman priest and she was failing to appease a faction who opposed female ordination. There was tension in the air. The flower ladies made the church look beautiful and the bell ringers rang the church bells. But my vicar's sermons told me that because of original sin, I was a bad person and God would send me to burn in Hell if I didn't repent. I remember thinking that most parishioners were happier not hearing this and were wise to stay at home.

But next Sunday I went to the Anglican cathedral to hear Bach's St Matthew Passion. It was performed by the cathedral boys choir and the Bach Society, and the great cathedral was packed to overflowing. The Gothic architecture was breathtaking and the stained-glass windows were radiant. The music of JS Bach reached out across the years and I concluded that if you wanted a spiritual experience in the Church of England, this was the place to find it.

That apart, it did not take too much effort to conclude that the Church of England is in a perilous state. For example:

• I read of a village which said recently that its Sunday tranquillity was disturbed by the church bells and they wanted them silenced.

• A report states that the Anglican Church is facing bankruptcy and the Archbishop of Canterbury is planning

to close half of all the parish churches in England.

- In the Anglican Church last year, 96% of its so-called members didn't go to church. Worse still, young people almost all say they are not interested in religion, and the next national census will allow them to identify themselves as individuals of no faith. At which point the membership of the Church of England will fall to zero.

- The Church of England was set up to please all religious beliefs, and in a changing landscape of faith, Queen Elizabeth I said she did not wish to build windows into men's souls. As a result, some of its theology became obscure, like the consecration of the bread and wine at Holy Communion. In the Roman Catholic Church, the position is clear and you must accept that the consecrated bread and wine are transubstantiated into the body and blood of Christ or leave the church. But in the Church of England the consecrated bread and wine remain bread and wine, but become an outward sign of the inner presence of God. Whatever that means.

- In the past, there were Recusancy Laws which compelled parishioners to attend church. But these were repealed in the 19th century and church attendances have steadily declined.

- In addition, congregations are now much better educated

and no longer believe the literal truth of the Bible, especially the New Testament gospels which were written many years after the death of Christ by writers who were not eye witnesses to the miracles they describe.

- Despite this, the church persists on preaching that the Bible is literally true, which has led to spreading disbelief and vanishing congregations.

- Children are no longer sent to Sunday School, and most schools no longer implement the 1944 Education Act, which says they must start each day with an act of Christian worship. As a result, few youngsters know the Bible stories and none go to church, except for baptisms, weddings and funerals.

- In the past, a Sabbath was observed on Sundays, to commemorate God's day of rest after he created the world. But nowadays the shops stay open, and many people go to work or to football matches, making the Sabbath feel like every other day of the week.

- Many churches can no longer find organists and choir masters to lead the congregational singing, and thus many church choirs have disbanded. As a result, the wonderful legacy of church music is in decline and hymn singing is no longer the experience it used to be, except on occasions like the Christmas service of Nine Lessons and Nine

Carols in Kings College Chapel.

- Security in churches has been increased because of theft, but despite security cameras, many have been stripped of their ornaments and cash collection boxes, and are now kept locked all day.

- There is a shortage of candidates for the ministry and some vicars now serve up to ten parishes, each of which once had their own vicar.

- In addition, theology colleges are accepting less qualified candidates and some vicars do not even seem to know their Bibles.

- Vicars no longer have significant community training as curates, but are launched on to the public almost as soon as they leave college. As a result, there are few of them who can deal with today's religious scepticism. And those like David Jenkins, the former Bishop of Durham who questioned the divinity of Christ and the resurrection, are threatened with expulsion.

- Weddings are declining and over 50% of marriages end in divorce. The Church now re-marries divorcees who have broken the vows they made before God and weddings for many couples are merely an excuse for an expensive party and a honeymoon holiday, paid for by the bride's father.

- In addition, less than 10% of funerals are now held along

religious lines and most are entirely secular.

- Homosexuality is forbidden in the Bible but is decriminalised throughout the western world. In Third World countries, however, it is condemned by the Church and some even support capital punishment of homosexuals. This is testing the world-wide Anglican Communion, and since some English vicars now bless same sex marriages, Third World bishops have boycotted the Lambeth Conference, and no longer recognise the Archbishop of Canterbury as their supreme head.

- There are bitter disputes within the Church hierarchy about women priests and bishops, and factions who say they will never accept them. Overlooking the importance of Mary Magdalene, some say that Christ's disciples were all men, and there must have been a reason for this. As a result, the Church has had to provide male counsellors for male priests who will not accept women in authority; they say it makes no difference that we live in a new age of gender equality, or that most people who go to church are women.

- Among the 42 diocesan bishops in England, the 26 most senior ones take turns to sit in the House of Lords. But there is opposition to unelected bishops participating in government and there are growing attempts to evict them,

including a national petition.

- The Church of England used to be the second largest landowner in the country and received vast rents from its properties but it now depends more on parish donations and many parishes are failing financially.

- Despite its looming bankruptcy, the Church is planning to spend £12m renovating the library at Lambeth Palace and £100m compensating the descendants of slaves it once owned on its Codrington and Cossitt slave plantations in Barbados.

- £125m is earmarked as compensation for the child victims of Church sex abuse. Hundreds of children have been sexually abused by priests, but most of these offences were concealed by those in authority. Only two priests from the whole world-wide communion have been convicted of child sex abuse and gaoled, both of them bishops.

- There has been a decline in Sunday Schools, and most of those started by Robert Raikes, which we attended just a generation ago, have closed through lack of support.

- As the Church struggles with long established issues like contraception and abortion, these are being overtaken by new problems such as gender dysphoria and assisted dying. The Anglican Church is failing to lead in all these ways,

whilst other churches like the Baptists and Pentecostals are flourishing, and non-Christian faiths like Islam and Buddhism are gaining converts. Worse still, secularists like Richard Dawkins are winning all the arguments about faith, and comedians like George Carlin are ridiculing the church on stage and on television.

As a result, the established Church is under serious threat whichever way it turns, and when King Charles III, the new Defender of the Faith, announced he would defend all faiths including no faith at all, some asked if an Archbishop, a Cardinal, a Rabbi or a Mullah should crown him, whether he would swear his coronation oath on the Holy Bible, the Talmud, the Quran or the Bhagavad Gita, and if his coronation should be held in Westminster Abbey.

The Church of England was created by Henry VIII to obtain a divorce from Catherine of Aragon so he could remarry and provide a male heir for the Tudor dynasty. It set Henry as its supreme head and stripped the Catholic monasteries of their vast wealth. The split from Rome and the Protestant Reformation may well have been inevitable, but my impression is that the Church of England has too many present-day problems and, unless it changes, it may not survive the next 50 years.

# 2. The Roman Catholics

*Pope Pius XII*

When choosing a Roman Catholic Church service, I particularly wanted to attend a Latin Mass. These were abolished by a Vatican Council in 1962, but after a public outcry there was a dispensation to use Latin if there was a local demand. As a result, Latin is still used from time to time in many Catholic churches and it adds to the state of mystery which is an important part of worship.

I went to morning Mass in the cathedral and the congregation was comprised mostly of Polish plumbers who had promised their mothers in Cracow and Gdansk that they would go to church whilst working in England.

When the time came for the priest to convert the bread into the body of Christ and the wine into blood, he covered them with a cloth napkin so no one could see the transubstantiation take place. When he raised the napkin, the plumbers gasped at the 'miracle' that had taken place. For my own part, I thought the bread still looked like bread, and, when the time came, it tasted like bread. But did I like the idea of a miracle and how those seated beside me believed it.

The authoritarian beliefs of Roman Catholicism are not for negotiation and if you don't accept them, you must cease to be a Roman Catholic. This appeals to those who don't want to struggle with the conundrums of belief. When I asked a Catholic friend how he dealt with the transubstantiation, he beamed from ear to ear and said, 'It's easy, my dear boy; we just don't talk about it.'

The Catholic Church has wonderful spectacles like the pilgrimages to Lourdes and Compostela whose proponents believe in miraculous cures for fatal illnesses that rely entirely on faith and are counter to scientific evidence. It believes in the assumption of the virgin Mary when the mother of Christ died

and ascended into heaven but there is no direct evidence of this, not even a description in the Bible; it was simply handed down by the Pope after what he described as a 'personal revelation'. But this sort of authoritarianism has its risks, and the Roman Catholic Church has made grave mistakes throughout its long history.

- The Roman Catholic Church launched the Crusades and the thousand-year wars between Christianity and Islam. It sanctioned the Spanish Inquisition and the treatment of heretics who it tortured and burned at the stake. As regards women, it allowed them to become nuns and join convents, and those who saw visions and performed miracles it canonised as saints. But an underlying fear of womanhood was never far from the surface, and whenever this broke through, women were labelled as witches and were drowned or burned at the stake.
- The Roman Catholic Church was deeply involved in the Atlantic slave trade and profited enormously from the proceeds, and, paradoxically, the nations it once enslaved are where Catholicism now succeeds the most.
- It supported anti-Semitic revenge against the Jews for killing Christ, and in WWII it did little to save the Hungarian and Italian Jews deported to Auschwitz-

Birkenau.

- To protect the treasures of the Vatican during WWII, it signed treaties with Hitler and Mussolini and it dissolved the German Catholic party to clear the way for Hitler's Nazis to come to power. Little wonder that when he celebrated Hitler's birthday, Pope Pius XII became known as 'Hitler's Pope'.

- The Roman Catholic Church convicted Galileo for asserting the earth was round and revolved around the sun. It took 300 years to admit its error and pardon him.

- The Catholic Church funded the medieval sacking of orthodox churches in Constantinople for not recognising the authority of the Pope.

- In modern times, it did nothing to prevent the massacres of Albanian Moslems or the genocide of Rwandan Tutsies.

- It still proposes a state of limbo for non-baptised children and it widely concealed the sexual abuse of school children by Catholic priests and bishops.

- In addition, it promoted the separation of unmarried mothers from their babies in Catholic mother and children homes.

- It continues to reject homosexuals within the clergy and insists on their celibacy.

- It canonised Mother Theresa despite her cruel withholding of pain killers from dying patients in the Calcutta Home for the Dying so they could experience the passion of Jesus Christ.

- And having forbidden contraception to limit the size of families, it forbids the use of condoms to prevent Aids.

- The Roman Catholic Church is the oldest and largest Christian Church in the world, comprising half of all Christians and a religious movement second only to Sunni Islam. In 313 AD, the Emperor Constantine ruled that the Roman Empire should relinquish the pagan religion of Mithras and adopt Christianity. Membership of the Roman Catholic Church grew to 1.3 billion, which is 18% of the world's population.

The Pope is head of the Roman Catholic church and the Curia is its governing authority in the Vatican City, which is the site of the **tomb of St Peter, its founder.** The position of **cardinal** is a rank of honour bestowed by popes on senior clerics, and the pope sometimes turns to the **College of Cardinals for advice.** After the pope's death, it is the cardinals who meet in an **electoral college in the Sistine Chapel** to elect his successor.

Catholic doctrine has developed over the centuries,

reflecting the teachings of Ecumenical Councils, Papal Bulls, and debates by Catholic scholars. In these matters, the Church believes it is guided by the Holy Spirit and is protected infallibly from doctrinal error. For example, in 1545, the Council of Trent developed a belief in the transubstantiation and in 1870 the First Vatican Council declared the pope infallible and the clergy were to be only males. Then in 1962, the Second Vatican Council abandoned the Latin Mass in favour of local languages.

Catholicism is based on the Trinity as set out in the Nicene Creed; Catholics believe that after death, our souls go to heaven, purgatory or hell. In addition, they believe that Mary, the mother of Jesus, remained a virgin throughout her life, conceived Christ by immaculate conception and ascended directly into heaven when she died.

The Catholic Church shared communion with the Eastern Orthodox Church until 1054 when there was a schism over the authority of the Pope, and in the 16th century, the sale of papal indulgences led to the Protestant Reformation of Martin Luther, who then had to hide from the Pope's assassins whilst he translated the Latin Bible into German. Without a male heir, Henry VIII of England petitioned the Pope to annul his marriage to Catherine of Aragon, and, when this was refused, Henry passed Acts of Supremacy which made him head of a

new Church of England, separated from Rome.

With the vast wealth gleaned from across Europe, the Catholic Church sponsored the best art, architecture and music, as well as employing Raphael, Michelangelo and Caravaggio to decorate their basilicas and palaces. Partly to protect them from Nazis like Herman Goering, the Holy See sought political neutrality in two World Wars but the Israeli historian Pinchas Lapide tells us that Pope Pius divulged German plans to the allies of V-1 flying bombs, V-2 rockets, Tiger tanks, and Messerschmitt jet fighters. In addition, some 2,500 Catholic clergy were sent to the Priest Barracks of Dachau concentration camp where many were tortured and murdered.

After World War II, Communist governments restricted religious freedoms and in 1949 the Communist victory in China led to the expulsion of foreign missionaries. Some priests who fell into the hands of the Communists were crucified. Karol Józef Wojtyła, Pope John Paul II, led the fight against Communist atheism in Eastern Europe, particularly in Poland where he was born.

The Catholic Church teaches that marriage is a social and spiritual bond between a man and a woman, and is the only context for sexual activity. Furthermore, a sacramental marriage, once consummated, cannot be dissolved except by death. The Catholic Church does not allow divorce or remarriage.

All forms of contraception are not permitted, although natural family planning is allowed so as to provide healthy spacing between births. The Catholic Church is the largest world provider of services to patients with HIV/AIDS, but there is controversy regarding the use of condoms to prevent new infections.

Similarly, the Catholic Church opposes artificial insemination to circumvent infertility, and vaccines derived from foetal cells obtained from abortions. It also teaches that homosexual acts are contrary to natural law, and opposes same-sex marriage.

Whilst Holy Orders are reserved for men, Catholic women have diverse roles in the life of the Church, and nuns have been widely involved in running the Church's health and education services. Efforts, however, to elevate women to the priesthood led the Curia to rule against it.

Finally, after many years of denial, the Catholic Church now recognises that sexual abuse of children took place under its aegis, and that it concealed what went on. But in 2014 Pope Francis instituted a Pontifical Commission for the Protection of Minors, and instruction to examine if priestly celibacy was a contributory cause.

The history of the Roman Catholic Church is a roller coaster of rulings, and its beliefs are now less followed in

developed countries. But the architecture of its basilicas and palaces are beautiful attractions to religious tourists. Its authoritarianism remains attractive to worshippers who do not want to wrestle with religious nuances.

# 3. The Methodists

*A Hedgerow Priest*

The Methodist Church was largely responsible for leading Christianity into the modern era but it was not easy and many Hedgerow Priests had to preach in the fields though many were

arrested and imprisoned. Nevertheless, John and Charles Wesley travelled around the countryside on horseback to preach, writing many of the hymns that are now sung in churches.

But there were only 15 in the congregation I attended, no organist to accompany the singing, and a stand-in priest from another town to conduct the service. In addition, the church was freezing cold and everyone was elderly.

Methodism began in the Church of England in the 18th century among a group of students at Oxford University who met to study the Bible. The first meetings outside the Church of England were launched in the 1730s. John and Charles Wesley took to open-air preaching and appointed fellow evangelists to travel the country after their fashion.

Methodist preachers were famous for their sermons, though some were accused of fanaticism, and Charles Wesley was nearly killed by a mob. As he and his assistants preached around the country, they formed local societies; as these multiplied, the breach with the Church of England widened. In 1784, Charles responded to the shortage of Anglican priests in the American colonies by ordaining Methodist preachers to administer the sacraments. In 1795, Methodist chapels were allowed to use his abridged *Book of Common Prayer* for baptisms and marriages.

Methodists were eventually excluded from the Church of England but their growth continued in the remote parts of Devon and Cornwall and in the mill towns of Yorkshire and Lancashire, where preachers taught that in the eyes of God, the working classes were equal to the upper classes. Or, as a 1793 epitaph reads on a memorial plaque outside a church in Devon:

'I lie here at the Chancel the door
Here lie I because I'm poor
The further in the more you pay
But I lie here as warm as they.'

The Methodist Conference became its governing body and John Wesley, its first president, wrote some 400 publications about theology, music, marriage, medicine, slavery and politics. But after his death it was decided that a new president would be elected each year, and Jabez Bunting, the next leader, allowed women into the church leadership. Mary Bosanquet and Sarah Crosby preached in orphanages and Selina Hastings, the Countess of Huntingdon, funded new chapels in England, and Trevecca College in Wales, where new ministers were trained. During the 20th century, Methodists adopted gender-neutral language in their Bible readings and one prayer was addressed to God Our Father and Mother which many found

challenging.

By 1837, there were 3000 Methodist Sunday Schools, 15,000 teachers and 340,000 pupils. The Methodist Conference gave its blessing for weekday schools and founded Westminster Teacher Training College. Membership grew to more than 40 million in 138 countries but declined when the Wesleyans split from the main body over the abolition of slavery.

Many signed a pledge against intoxicating liquors, and Methodism remains closely associated with the Temperance movement. In 1869, a Methodist dentist called Thomas Welch developed a pasteurised grape juice for use as unfermented Communion wine.

Modern Methodists like Donald Soper promoted pacifism and nuclear disarmament and were elected to the House of Lords and a Methodist called Margaret Thatcher became Britain's first female prime minister. The Methodist Church opposes abortion, assisted suicide and euthanasia, and supported the campaign to abolish capital punishment. But it blesses same-sex relationships, allows the ordination of gay ministers and permits transgender members to marry.

In these ways, the Methodist Church did much to advance Christianity in the modern world and whilst the church I visited was struggling, I am told of others which are not, and I wish them well.

# 4. The Pentecostal Church

*Tongues of Fire*

There was so much about Pentecostalism I looked forward to, not least the speaking with tongues of fire and their faith healing. But there were none of these at the service I attended which was disappointing.

After the crucifixion and resurrection of Jesus Christ, the disciples gathered in Jerusalem for the Jewish harvest festival, which is celebrated seven weeks after the Festival of Passover. At the Feast of Pentecost, the New Testament says there was a mighty rushing wind and tongues of fire: the disciples were filled with the Holy Spirit, and began to speak in other tongues as the Spirit gave them utterance. Some scholars interpret the passage as a reference to the multitude of languages spoken by the gathered crowds, while others say that it meant the apostles had found their courage at last and were speaking in ecstasy.

The movement emerged during the time of 19th-century evangelism in America where it was believed the second coming of Christ was imminent.

Benjamin Simpson and his Christian Missionary Alliance built Assemblies of God. John Alexander Dowie and Maria Woodworth Etter joined as faith healers. Charles Fox Parham started a Bible school in Topeka, Kansas, where he taught that speaking in tongues was proof of receiving the Holy Spirit. And in England, Alexander Boddy, the Anglican vicar of All Saints Church in Sunderland, became the founder of British Pentecostalism. Others took the revival to India, Hong Kong, West Africa and South Africa. T.B. Barratt started the Pentecostal movement in Sweden, Norway and Denmark, and Germaigi Francesconi established congregations in Argentina

and Brazil. According to some sources, Pentecostalism is still the fastest-growing religious movement, and in 1995 it was estimated there were 217 million Pentecostals throughout the world, particularly in sub-Saharan Africa and Central and South America.

The movement soon became associated with the impoverished and the marginalized, especially black Americans. Pentecostals called for the abolition of racial segregation and the Jim Crow Laws, which eventually gave rise to the modern Civil Rights Movement. From the outset, women were assigned equal rights, and those like Agnes Ozman served as pastors, wrote hymns, edited newsletters and taught in Bible schools. However, some groups continued to observe a secondary role for women and insisted they should wear head coverings.

Some groups supported the Temperance Movement, rejected the use of wine at Communion, and used grape juice instead. The majority of early churches taught pacifism and conscientious objection to war, which brought them into conflict with authority. As a result, during WWII, many in Germany were sent to Nazi concentration camps.

Some groups practised foot washing in deference to the humility of Christ, and embraced the prohibition of dancing, abstinence from tobacco, and modest dress codes.

Pentecostals believe that baptism is an outward symbol of an inner conversion, and most groups practise baptism by immersion. They believe that baptism means being made part of the body of the Church and repentance of sin and being born again are fundamental requirements to receive it. Because they regarded speaking in tongues as a universal language, missionaries no longer bothered to learn the languages of those they evangelized; some claimed to speak foreign languages they had never even heard. But when they did speak in tongues, they spoke unintelligibly and were dubbed by outsiders as demons. As a result, many who underwent Pentecostal baptism kept it private and many remained within their original churches and were known as Neo-Pentecostals. Nowadays, speaking in tongues is no longer common among Pentecostals, and in 2006, a ten-country survey found that 49 percent never prayed in tongues.

A simultaneous development was a Divine Healing Revival led by William Branham. This is performed by anointing with oil and laying on of hands, or by handing out healing cloths over which prayers have been said. During the early years, Pentecostals thought it was sinful to consume medicine from doctors and to this day, some rely exclusively on prayer and divine healing. Some churches have advised their members against vaccination, stating this is for those who are weak in

faith and that with a confession of sins, they would be immune from disease. But when some parents relied on faith healing for their children and the children died, the courts became involved and some parents were convicted and sent to gaol.

Pentecostals teach that any spirit-filled Christian has the potential to prophesy but whilst a prophetic utterance might foretell future events, this is not its primary purpose. And it must never to be used for personal guidance, as prophetic utterances are subject to error.

I had very much wanted to see some of these practices and would have loved to hear what speaking in tongues of fire sounded like. But it was not to be and I had to watch it on YouTube.

# 5. The Baptist Church

*Baptism by Immersion*

The Baptist church I attended was packed to overflowing, and was by far the most enjoyable of all the services I went to. Noisy children ran around looking for hidden jars of sweets, and teenagers were canoodling in the rear pews. And when a rock and roll band struck up, everyone stood and started clapping. I had never realised that so much church music had been set to rock and roll, and that performers like Paul Baloche and Brenton Brown are international stars.

The involvement of the congregation was how I remember church services as a boy and, leaving at the end of the service, one of the door keepers turned out to be my own GP. When he spotted me, he beamed from ear to ear and asked if I'd enjoyed myself, which I had. He said if I came next week, they would be uncovering the baptismal pool in front of the altar and some new members were going to be baptised.

I think church services will have to be more entertaining if they are to attract big congregations again, especially youngsters. I would have loved the St Thomas Kirche in Leipzig where J.S. Bach wrote a new cantata for them every Sunday and the services lasted all morning. My local Baptist Church in 2020 was not Leipzig in 1740, but I went away having glimpsed again the church worship of my boyhood, and I loved it.

Conservatives within the wider Church say the Christian message is a serious matter, and there is no place for happy-clappy populism. But others think the church must move with the times, and whilst Brenton Brown is not J.S. Bach, I think the great master would have approved of him.

Baptist churches trace their history to the English Separatist movement in the 1600s, when some Christians were unhappy with the slow progress of the Protestant Reformation.

In 1579 in Poland, Faustus Socinus introduced adult

baptism by immersion. Baptist churches were started in England by John Smythe in 1609. They believed the Bible was the only guide to a true belief in Christ, and adult baptism was the form the scriptures described. Also, infants would not be damned if they died before they were baptised as adults. When Smythe died, Thomas Helwys took over the leadership, and he founded the first General Baptist Church in east London in 1612. In 1638, John Spilsbury adopted the practice of adult baptism by total immersion. Roger Williams and John Clarke are credited with founding the earliest Baptist church in North America in 1639 in Providence Rhode Island. This energized the Baptist movement, which then underwent spectacular growth.

In the USA, Baptists became the largest Christian communities in the south, and included the enslaved Black population. In 1845, Baptist Conventions in the north and south split over slavery but by 2015, American Baptists numbered 50 million and constituted one-third of all American Protestants.

Most Baptists call for freedom from oversight and control, except for the Episcopalians who still have governing elders. In matters of sexuality, many Baptist churches promote a virginity pledge and young Baptists are exhorted towards sexual abstinence until Christian marriage.

In late 18th century USA, Black free men began to organise separate churches. Black state conventions were set up in southern states and Black preachers interpreted the US Civil War as God's gift to Black freedom. But the Baptist Convention still supported barriers to Black voter registration and racial segregation under the Jim Crow Laws. When Baptist deacon Samuel Sharpe organised a general strike of 60,000 slaves seeking better lives, it became known as the Baptist War, and was put down by government troops. An estimated 200 slaves were killed, and 300 more were judicially executed.

The Baptist church I went to was by far the best attended, and there must have been close to 1000 in the congregation. The service was the most enjoyable of any I went to. I see no reason why churches shouldn't be happy places for congregations to enjoy their Sunday worship, and when the fall-out worsens in other churches, I expect the Baptists to flourish.

# 6. The Spiritualist Church

*A Table Séance*

The Spiritualist church I attended was like a village hall, with rows of stacking chairs and a raised dais with a lectern. It was completely full and more chairs had to be found to accommodate latecomers.

I had never been before and I knew no one in the

congregation, and no one was aware I was attending that day. So, I was shocked when the pastor asked from the lectern, 'Is there a new member of the congregation, called Brian?' I sheepishly raised my hand and she said, 'I have a message, is it from Elizabeth?' (My deceased wife.) Aghast, I nodded. 'She says to tell you that she is watching over you, and don't forget to feed the cat.'

Like most of the congregation around me, I was a bereaved spouse who was curious for any contact with a deceased loved one. But I have no idea how the pastor knew I was going to her service that day, let alone my name, nor that my wife was Elizabeth and that she had died recently. But somehow she had discovered these facts, and to this day I don't know how. She was wrong about the cat, however; I don't have a cat and I've never had one.

The origin of Spiritualism was linked to the séances conducted by the Fox sisters in Hydesville, New York around 1848. By 1853, the movement reached London, and by 1860 it was worldwide. Other notable Spiritualists of that era were Mercy Cadwallader, who became a missionary, and Emma Hardinge Britten, who wrote for the Yorkshire Spiritual Telegraph, the first Spiritualist newspaper in Britain.

In 1891, the National Federation of Spiritualists (NFS) was founded and grew quickly before its name was changed to the

Spiritualists National Union (or SNU). The British Spiritualists were often adherents of the temperance and anti-capital punishment lobbies, and were frequently vegetarians. Some advocated women's rights and female suffrage, and some espoused free love.

Two Worlds was another British Spiritualism magazine with a large circulation, which advertised the contact details of local séance circles. One of the renowned mediums of his era was a man called D.D. Home who did much to make Spiritualism fashionable among the upper classes. Trance mediums flourished and table turning became popular, reputedly even in Buckingham Palace.

In 1932, another magazine, Psychic News, began carrying news of local Spiritualist churches, and nowadays there are on-line websites. From 1920 to 1938, there was a British College of Psychic Studies founded by a Mr. and Mrs. Mackenzie in London, and an Arthur Findlay College at Stansted which continues to this day. Other Spiritualist groups in the UK included the White Eagle Lodge, the Institute of Spiritualist Mediums, and the Noah's Ark Society, whose focus was on training new mediums.

There are now Spiritualist churches throughout the world and the ISF holds congresses every two years. Their church services are conducted by a medium with an opening prayer,

an address to the congregation, the singing of hymns, and, finally, a demonstration of mediumship. Spiritual healing may also be part of the proceedings.

Some Spiritualists maintain that Spiritualism is a religion in its own right, whilst others say it's a denomination within the Christian Church. It is variously described as a philosophy, a science, a religion, or a way of life. Spiritualists believe that when people die, an aspect of their mind survives and continues to exist in a <u>spirit world</u>. One purpose of a medium is to provide evidence of this, and the accuracy with which the deceased are remembered helps convince living relatives and friends that the medium has had contact with their spirit.

Mediums develop their ability by sitting regularly in circles with other psychics. Meditation plays a large role in this. Spiritualist healing during church services is a form of mediumship which is said to direct healing energy to the patient from a higher source. The healer uses his or her laying-on of hands to heal diseased body parts. But when the parents of sick children have depended entirely on this, and the children have died, some parents have been convicted in court and imprisoned.

Among the most famous practitioners is the writer, magistrate, farmer and businessman Arthur Findlay who left his mansion as a place for the study and advancement of psychic

science. This is now a Psychic College in Stansted and is run by the SNU. In addition, a clairvoyant called Helen Duncan achieved notoriety in 1941 when she revealed the Royal Navy's HMS Barham had just been torpedoed and sunk. This was not public knowledge and there was concern that if she was a genuine clairvoyant, she could disclose secrets to the enemy. As a result, Churchill ordered her arrested, imprisoned and forbidden from holding séances again.

Mediumship gained in popularity during the nineteenth century when Ouija boards became commonly used. Various notables like Arthur Conan Doyle were persuaded to believe in Spiritualism.

In explanation, some psychologists implicated the hypnotism of over-receptive subjects, and noted that Spiritualism attracted adherents with strong interests in social justice, especially women. As a result, some mediums delivered impassioned sermons about the abolition of slavery, abstention from alcohol, and women's suffrage.

But whenever scientific investigations tried to explain how mediumship worked, almost all revealed fraud, with many mediums employing the techniques of stage magicians. As a result, most mediumship is presented in a darkened room where mediums can use spirit cabinets and levitation tables without too much scrutiny. Ectoplasm emitting from a

medium's mouth was achieved by using cheese cloth concealed in the mouth and there is much made of secret eavesdropping, and searching telephone directories and obituary columns in newspapers. Many mediums eventually confess their deceptions but others persist in false claims, and some have even been imprisoned for fraud.

I found my own experience quite inexplicable and I ended up focusing on how they achieved it, rather than the content. As the medium didn't reveal anything interesting about other deceased relatives in the congregation, and there was no faith healing, I didn't go again.

# 7. The Scientologists

*An Electro-Psychometer*

I was invited for an interview in a Church of Scientology office in a former High Street shop, for them to ascertain if I was suitable to join them. They said I needed to confirm I believed in God and they asked me to read aloud the Nicene Creed whilst holding the electrodes of an electro-psychometer, which is a sort of lie detector. But as I read, "I believe in God the Father Almighty, Maker of Heaven and Earth," the lights on the

machine started flashing and the needle on the dial started waving back and forth. At this point, they turned it off and said I had failed the test and they were sorry to have to turn me away. So, I never got to the Friday church service in the back of the shop, or a wedding, a child naming, or a funeral which was disappointing as the Church of Scientology turned out to be the most intriguing of all the churches I attended. An atheist friend who was with me rather annoyingly passed the lie detector test with flying colours.

The Church of Scientology was founded by Ron L. Hubbard who was born in the USA in 1911 and spent three terms at George Washington University until he was placed on probation and sent down. During **WWII**, he was commissioned into the US Navy, but his claimed sinking of an enemy submarine was questioned and he was court marshalled and lost his command. Reporting stomach pains, he spent the rest of the war in hospital where he asked the Veterans Administration for psychiatric treatment.

In 1951, his wife consulted doctors who recommended he be committed to a psychiatric hospital for treatment of paranoid schizophrenia and from then on he condemned psychiatry as evil, barbaric and corrupt.

In 1945, he lived in Pasadena with Alistair Crawley, the English leader of an Occult sect called Ordo Templi Orientis.

He practised as a hypnotist in Hollywood and posed as a swami. This experience led him to create Dianetics as a form of psychotherapy and his book on this subject was published in a pulp magazine as a counselling technique to help deal with past traumatic events. The book spent six months on the New York Times best seller list, but the Journal of the American Medical Association dismissed it out of hand. Newsweek said it was not even worth discussing. In addition, many said Dianetics were a form of hypnosis and could be dangerous.

In 1951, a Board of Medical Examiners sued the Dianetics Foundation for teaching medicine without a license, and at this point Hubbard proposed that Scientology should become a religion, especially since there were tax advantages for doing so. There followed an era of conflict with the police and the courts in different countries, as well as with their governments. In 1963, US Food and Drug Administration agents raided Hubbard's offices, seizing hundreds of E-meters as illegal medical devices, and tons of literature which they said made false medical claims. As a result, the US courts ordered the organisation to label the meters as religious artefacts, to post a $20,000 bond of compliance, and to pay the FDA's legal expenses.

Since then, the Church has been in conflict with governments and police forces in the USA, UK, Canada,

France, Germany and Australia. It is one of the most litigious organisations in history, filing countless lawsuits. And it famously proclaimed that Scientology is not a turn-the-other-cheek religion.

Allegations have been repeated that the Church of Scientology is an unscrupulous commercial enterprise which exploits its members and encourages them to shun any friends or family who are antagonistic. And more recently, Scientology has used private investigators and former police officers to protect its interests.

During the 1970s, some of Hubbard's followers infiltrated the US government, and several were convicted and imprisoned for it. Hubbard himself was convicted of fraud by a French court in 1978 and sentenced to four years in prison, but fled. Then in 1979, following FBI raids, 11 senior members in the organisation were convicted of obstructing justice, burglary of US government offices, and theft of documents. In 1992, a court in Canada convicted the organisation of spying on law enforcement and government agencies, and in the UK in 1999, the Charity Commission ruled that Scientology was not a religion and refused to register it as a charity.

The Church of Scientology is one of the wealthiest in the world with revenues of $200 million a year. But in 2009,

Senator Nick Xenophon in a speech to the Australian Federal Parliament alleged it was a criminal organisation and it was banned from Australia.

But its global spread continued and included the opening of offices in Johannesburg and Paris, and a world headquarters in Surrey where Hubbard came to live for seven years. But in 1972, facing criminal charges, he fled back to the USA to live in New York before going into hiding where his only contacts with the outside world were ten trusted messengers, and excluded even his wife. Then in 1980, he disappeared and later died on a ranch in California in 1986.

Scientologists believe that all humans are immortal, spiritual beings they call Thetans, who reside inside earthly human bodies. Thetans have spent past lives_in an extra-terrestrial culture called Xenu and are reborn time and time again into new bodies through a process of reincarnation. Scientology proposes a relationship between earlier incarnations and the present life, with Thetans becoming stronger with each rebirth.

Also, there was a ruler of a confederation of planets who, 75 million years ago, brought alien beings to Earth in a spacecraft and then killed them all with thermonuclear weapons. Following this, Thetans clustered into the dead bodies of human beings. They also say that Thetan memories go back 76 trillion years, which is much longer than the age of

the universe.

Scientology aims for a civilisation without insanity, crime or war, and where honest human beings are free to prosper. It has no dogma concerning God and does not ask individuals to accept anything on faith alone. They believe that as one's spiritual awareness increases, one attains a deeper relationship with the Supreme Being. The Church of Scientology holds that its higher mystical teachings may be harmful to the unprepared and must be kept from those who have not yet reached higher levels of understanding. These teachings include the cosmic catastrophes that befell the Thetans. Scientology also asserts some people are malevolent, and 20 percent of the population have suppressed antisocial personalities which are dangerous, for example, Adolph Hitler and Genghis Khan, as well as serial murderers and drug traffickers.

In 1966, Hubbard formed a ship-based sea Organisation called Sea Org which operated three cruise ships: the *Diana*, the *Athena*, and the *Apollo*. The Church's hierarchy became members of Sea Org-including 5,000 of their most dedicated adherents, who worked for low pay and sign a billion-year contract. Sea Org members were not permitted to raise children on the ships and some pregnant women say they were pressured into undergoing abortions.

The organisation also operates the Scientology Archiving

Project, which preserves the works of Hubbard on stainless steel tablets, encased in titanium capsules in specially constructed vaults around the world.

Hubbard also created a list of celebrities targeted for conversion to Scientology, and to popularize it. It operates eight Celebrity Centres, the largest of which is in Hollywood, California, with film stars like Gloria Swanson, Tom Cruise, John Travolta and Goldie Hawn.

Its Narconon organisation promotes Hubbard's theories about substance abuse and drug addiction, and its Criminon organisation introduces Scientology to criminals in prisons. Its Applied Scholastics organisation teaches Scientology to school students and operates private schools throughout the United States, including a flagship academy in Yamhill, Oregon. Its World Institute of Scientology spreads Scientology to the business sector and its Way to Happiness promotes a moral code written by Hubbard, which has been translated into more than 40 languages. In addition, there is an International Association of Scientologists, which opposes oppressive governments and police agencies such as Interpol.

But I was denied access to all these aspects of the faith as I failed to pass the lie detector test on my first visit!

# 8. The Unitarians

*The Trinity*

In the tiny Unitarian church I went to, there were just a dozen in the congregation. The service was bland, and what I imagined a committee meeting of the Communist party might be like. When they served refreshments after the service, the tea was cold and the cake was stale.

Their *raison d'être* is their opposition to the Trinity of Father, Son and Holy Ghost. As a result, they believe Christ was inspired by God but was not God himself.

The divinity of Christ greatly troubled early Christians, and the opponents in the debate were led by Athenasius of Alexandria and Arius of Cyrenea. Then, in 313 AD the Emperor Constantine convened the Conference of Nicea, and adopted the Trinity to resolve this schism in the Eastern churches. It is against Constantine's perceived corruption of original Christianity that modern Unitarians are opposed.

The movement began in Poland in the 16th century among Italians taking refuge from the Roman Catholic Church. The Polish Brethren were born out of a controversy in 1556 when Piotr Goniadz, a Polish student, spoke out against the Trinity. In 1565, these anti-Trinitarians were excluded from the Catholic synod and they began to hold their own meetings and adopt the views of Fausto Sozzini.

But then in 1658, they were disbanded and ordered to convert to Roman Catholicism. Most of them fled to Transylvania or Holland. The movement became popular in England and in 1774 Theophilus Lindsay organised meetings with Joseph Priestley and the Lunar Society.

In England, their first church was established in 1774 in Essex Street, London, where today's headquarters are still located, and Unitarian communities developed around the world. In the United States, James Freeman began teaching Unitarianism and in 1786 he revised *The Book of Common Prayer*

according to Unitarian doctrines.

Unitarians charge that the Trinity fails to adhere to strict monotheism, and they maintain that Jesus was a great man and a prophet, but was not God. And they point out that Jesus did not claim to be God and his teachings did not suggest a Trinity. Fausto Sozzini believed that Jesus Christ began his life when he was born as a human, was not conceived by the Holy Spirit, nor did he become the Son of God. In rejecting the virgin birth, Unitarians question the historical accuracy of the Bible. Worship within the Unitarian tradition accommodates a wide range of understandings, and each congregation is at liberty to devise its own beliefs and style of worship.

The current president of the Unitarian Universal Association is Reverend Susan Frederick Gray. Notable Unitarians include Bela Bartok, Ralph Waldo Emerson, Elizabeth Gaskell, Frank Lloyd Wright and Josiah Wedgwood. Seven Nobel Prizes have been awarded to Unitarians, and four presidents of the United States were Unitarians, including Thomas Jefferson.

In the United Kingdom, Unitarianism had a huge impact on Victorian politics, and Unitarian families became prominent in the social and political life of Britain, including the Wollstoncrofts, the Nettlefolds, the Martineaus, the Luptons, the Kitsons, the Chamberlains and the Kenricks. Notable

individuals include Sir Tim Berners Lee, the inventor of the World Wide Web, Lancelot Ware, the founder of Mensa, and Sir Adrian Boult, the music conductor.

All this seems fundamental to how modern Christians regard Christ, and in a world now sceptical about his divinity, Unitarianism might be one of the ways for Christianity to survive.

# 9. Jehovah's Witnesses

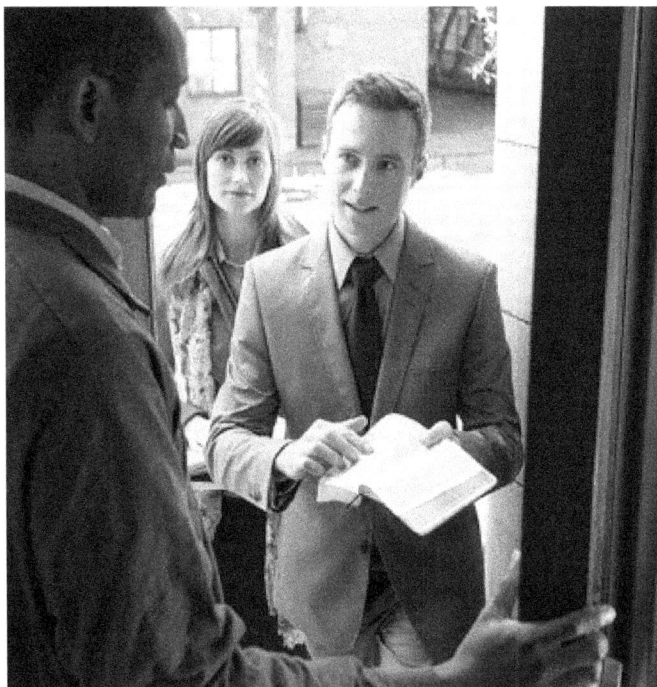

*Doorstep Evangelism*

At a Jehovah's Witness service in their Kingdom Hall, the highpoint was an hour-long Bible study, led by an elder. The Bible passage had been selected the previous week and a lady

seated beside me had worked hard and made copious notes. The rest of the service comprised prayers and hymn singing, and there was a large congregation.

Most of us meet the Jehovah's Witnesses when they turn up on our door step to leave a copy of their *Watchtower* magazine. Their origins and history are interesting. In 1870, Charles Russell formed a group in Pittsburgh Pennsylvania to study the Bible. During his ministry, Russell disputed many beliefs of mainstream Christianity including the immortality of the soul, hell fire, bodily resurrection, the Trinity, and the apocalypse. In 1876, Russell met Nelson Barbour and that year they published the *Three Worlds* magazine which taught that world society would be replaced by the establishment of God's kingdom on earth. In 1878, Russell and Barbour published the *Herald of the Morning*, and followed this in 1879 with *Zion's Watchtower* and *The Herald of Christ's Presence* in which they argued that the world was in its last days, and a new age under the reign of Jesus Christ was imminent.

From 1879, *Watchtower* supporters began gathering in their own congregations to study the Bible and Russell visited each congregation to ensure the format of their meetings. By 1900, he had organised thousands of colporteurs and missionaries, and he had established branch offices. Furthermore, he had nearly a hundred travelling preachers by 1910. He also engaged

in major publishing efforts, and by 1912 he was the most read Christian author in the USA.

In 1909, Russell moved the *Watchtower* headquarters to New York, and volunteers were housed in a nearby residence they called Bethel. He called the movement The International Bible Students Association and by 1910 about 50,000 people worldwide were members; these congregations re-elected him annually as their leader. He died in 1916 on a ministerial speaking tour and Joseph Rutherford succeeded him. But divisions between supporters triggered a turnover of members over the next decade.

In 1917, Rutherford released *The Finished Mystery* which strongly criticized the Catholic and Protestant clergy in the Great War and, as a result, some Watchtower Society directors were jailed for sedition.

Rutherford appointed a director in each congregation, and members were instructed to report their activity to the Brooklyn headquarters. Then, at an international convention in Cedar Point, Ohio, in 1922, a new emphasis was placed on house-to-house preaching. Significant changes in doctrine were introduced during Rutherford's 25 years as president, including an announcement that the Hebrew patriarchs Abraham and Isaac would be resurrected in 1925, which would mark the beginning of Christ's earthly kingdom. But these predictions

passed unfulfilled, and tens of thousands of defections followed. Then in 1931, at a convention in Columbus, Ohio, he introduced the new name, Jehovah's Witnesses, which was drawn from Isaiah 43:10: 'Ye are my witnesses, saith the Lord, and my servant whom I have chosen.'

From 1932, Rutherford explained that in addition to the 144,000 anointed who would be resurrected to live in heaven and rule over the earth with Christ, a separate class of members, the great multitude, would live in a paradise restored on earth. From 1935, new converts to the movement were considered part of that class.

As their interpretations of the Bible evolved, their publications decreed that saluting national flags was a form of idolatry, and this led to mob violence and government suppression. Despite this, by Rutherford's death in 1942, worldwide membership reached 113,600 and there were 5,300 congregations.

Nathan Knorr was appointed next president of the Watchtower Society in 1942, and commissioned a new translation of the Bible called *The New World Translation of the Holy Scriptures*, the full version of which was released in 1961. He organised international assemblies, implemented new training programs, and expanded missionary activity and branch offices throughout the world. Knorr's presidency was

also marked by instructions to guide Witnesses in their conduct and procedures to enforce a strict moral code.

From 1966, Witness publications built up anticipation that Christ's earthly reign would begin in 1975. The number of baptisms increased and by 1975, the number of members exceeded two million. But then these expectations were unfulfilled and membership declined again.

Elders were restored to congregations in 1975 and it was announced that their appointments would be made by travelling overseers. In 1976, the power of the Watch Tower Society president was passed to the governing body. Since Knorr's death in 1977, the position of president has been occupied by Frederick Franz and Milton Hensche. In 1995, Jehovah's Witnesses abandoned the idea that Armageddon would occur during the lives of the generation alive in 1914.

The UK governing body based in their Warwick headquarters is an all-male group comprised of eight members, with support staff living in properties owned by the organisation. The living expenses of full-time employees are covered by the organisation, along with a basic monthly stipend. New elders are appointed by a travelling overseer after recommendation by the existing body of elders. Ministerial servants, appointed in a similar manner, fulfil clerical and attendant duties, and may teach and help conduct meetings.

Elders maintain responsibility for governance, meeting times, speakers and agendas, directing the public preaching work, and creating committees to investigate misconduct or doctrinal breaches.

Baptism is required to be a member of Jehovah's Witnesses but they do not practise infant baptism, and baptisms performed by other denominations are not considered valid. Their literature emphasises how members must be obedient and loyal to Jehovah, and they must remain part of the organisation to survive Armageddon.

The Watch Tower Society has produced over 227 million Bible copies of *The New World Translation*, in over 185 languages. In 2010, the *Watchtower* and *Awake* were the most widely distributed magazines in the world. Translation of Witness publications is done by 2,000 volunteers worldwide, and the literature appears in most languages, as hard copy and on internet websites. Much of their funding is provided by donations, primarily from members and the Watch Tower Society is one of New York's richest corporations.

Jehovah's Witnesses believe they are the restoration of first century Christianity and that doctrinal refinements result from revelation, via reason and study. The Society also teaches that members of the governing body are helped by the Holy Spirit to discern deep truths, which are then considered by the

governing body before it makes its decisions.

Jehovah's Witnesses consider the Bible is scientifically and historically accurate, and interpret much of it literally, believing it to be the final authority for all their beliefs, although Watch Tower Society publications also carry some weight. Regular personal Bible reading is recommended, but Witnesses are discouraged from personal doctrines and are cautioned against reading other religious literature. The organisation makes no provision for members to criticise official teachings.

They believe Jesus died on a single upright post rather than the traditional cross and that he was resurrected as a spirit, and only assumed human form for a temporary period after his resurrection. Jehovah's Witnesses believe that Satan was a perfect angel who developed self-importance and craved worship, influencing Adam and Eve to disobey God, and that the other angels who sided with Satan became demons. Jehovah's Witnesses teach that Satan and his demons were cast down to earth from heaven on 1st October 1914 and that Satan is the ruler of the current world order and the cause of all human suffering.

Witnesses believe that a group of 144,000 selected humans go to heaven, and rule with Jesus as kings over the earth, and this kingdom is the means by which God accomplishes his purpose on earth, transforming it into a paradise without

sickness or death. They believe the kingdom was established in heaven in 1914 and that Jehovah's Witnesses serve as representatives of the kingdom on earth. They consider all other religions to be false, and believe they will soon be destroyed. After Armageddon, God will extend his heavenly kingdom and the earth will be transformed into a paradise like the Garden of Eden. Jehovah's Witnesses believe that Jesus Christ began to rule in heaven, as king of God's kingdom, in October 1914, and that Satan was subsequently ousted from heaven to earth, resulting in all the misery of humanity.

Jehovah's Witnesses believe that women were designed by God for a complementary role to men but women can participate in public preaching and work at Bethel. Women may also profess to be members of the 144,000, but only men are allowed to hold positions of authority. Congregational elders are exclusively male positions and women are not allowed to address the congregation except if there are no eligible men, and then they must wear a head covering. Congregations meet for two sessions each week and their most solemn event is the commemoration of Christ's death on the day of the Jewish Passover.

Jehovah's Witnesses are best known for their evangelism, most notably visiting people from house to house and distributing literature from the Watchtower Society. The

objective is to start a regular Bible study with any person who is not a member, with the intention that the student will be baptised and join them. Witnesses are advised to discontinue Bible studies with students who show no interest in becoming members and they are to devote as much time as possible to their ministry, and submit monthly Field Service Reports.

All sexual relations outside of marriage are grounds for expulsion. Homosexual activity is considered a serious sin, and same-sex marriages are forbidden. Abortion is considered murder and suicide is considered to be self-murder and a sin against God. Modesty in dress is emphasized. Gambling, drunkenness, illegal drugs, and tobacco are forbidden. Drinking alcoholic beverages on the other hand is permitted in moderation.

Within families, the husband has authority over family decisions, but is encouraged to solicit his wife's thoughts and feelings, as well as those of his children. Marriages must be monogamous and legally registered, and marrying a non-believer carries religious sanctions. Divorce is discouraged, and remarriage is forbidden unless the divorce is for adultery. If a divorce is obtained for any other reason, remarriage is considered adulterous unless there was sexual immorality, physical abuse or non-support of one's family.

Formal discipline is administered by congregational elders

when a judicial committee is formed to determine guilt. This can lead to the subject being dis-fellowshipped. And Witnesses are taught that avoiding interaction with such individuals helps keep the congregation free from immorality.

Jehovah's Witnesses believe that the Bible condemns the mixing of religions, and there can only be one truth from God. They reject interfaith and ecumenical movements. They also believe that only Jehovah's Witnesses represent true Christianity, and that other religions will soon be destroyed. Attending university is discouraged, as receiving any higher education is considered dangerous.

Jehovah's Witnesses remain politically neutral, do not seek public office, and are discouraged from voting, though they can participate in uncontroversial community issues. They should respect the authority of the governments under which they live. They do not celebrate religious holidays such as Christmas and Easter, nor do they observe birthdays, national holidays, or other celebrations that honour people other than Jesus. They feel these and other customs have pagan origins or reflect a political spirit. In this respect, their position is that traditional holidays reflect Satan's control over the world. Witnesses are told that spontaneous giving at other times can help children not to feel deprived of birthdays or other celebrations.

They do not work in industries associated with the military and they refuse military service, which in some countries results in their arrest and imprisonment. They do not salute or pledge allegiance to flags, or sing national anthems or patriotic songs. And Jehovah's Witnesses see themselves as a worldwide brotherhood which transcends national boundaries.

Jehovah's Witnesses refuse blood transfusions, which they consider a violation of Acts 15;28. And since 1961, the willing acceptance of a blood transfusion by an unrepentant member has been grounds for expulsion from the group. Members are directed to refuse blood transfusions, even in life-or-death situations, though they can accept non-blood alternatives and undergo medical procedures without blood transfusions. Their literature provides information about non-blood transfusion supported medical procedures. Jehovah's Witnesses do not accept the transfusion of whole blood, packed red cells, platelets, white cells or plasma. Autologous blood donation, where an individual's own blood is stored for later use, is also unacceptable. The Watchtower Society provides pre-formatted power of attorney documents, prohibiting major blood components, in which members can specify which treatments they will personally accept. And Hospital Liaison Committees have been established as a cooperative arrangement between Jehovah's Witnesses and the medical professions.

They have an active presence in most countries, but do not form a large part of the population of any of them. In 2021, Jehovah's Witnesses reported 8.7 million members involved in preaching, and over 1.4 billion hours spent doing this.

Controversy surrounding their various beliefs has led to opposition from governments, communities, and other religious groups. And Jehovah's Witnesses are the most persecuted Christians of the twentieth century. Their stance regarding political neutrality and their refusal to serve in the military led to the imprisonment of members who refused conscription during World War II, and at other times when national service became compulsory. Their religious activities are currently banned in China, Russia, Vietnam and in many Muslim countries.

In 1933, there were approximately 20,000 Jehovah's Witnesses in Nazi Germany, of whom about 10,000 were imprisoned because they refused allegiance to Hitler. Of those, 2,000 were sent to Nazi concentration camps (where they were identified by purple triangles), and 1,200 died, of whom 250 were executed. In socialist East Germany, from 1950 to 1980, Jehovah's Witnesses were persecuted extensively by the Stasi. In 1951, about 9,300 Witnesses in the Soviet Union were deported to the Gulag Archipelago in Siberia. Then in 2017, the Supreme Court of Russia labelled Jehovah's Witnesses as

an extremist organisation, banned its activities and confiscated its assets.

Jehovah's Witnesses have received criticism from mainstream Christianity, and the movement has been accused of doctrinal inconsistency and reversals, failed predictions, mis-translation of the Bible, harsh treatment and coercive leadership. Criticism has often focused on their rejection of blood transfusions, particularly in life-threatening medical situations.

They have been accused of a culture that conceals cases of sexual abuse within their organisation; they have been criticised for their two-witness rule, which requires sexual abuse to be supported by secondary evidence, and if it is not, the elders must leave the matter in Jehovah's hands. Their failure to report abuse allegations to the legal authorities has also been criticised although the Watchtower Society's policy is for elders to inform the civil authorities when required by law to do so. In court cases, the Watchtower Society has been found negligent in the protection of children from known sex offenders and has settled child abuse lawsuits out of court, reportedly paying $780,000 to one plaintiff without admitting wrong doing. In 2017, the UK Charity Commission began an inquiry into Jehovah's Witnesses' handling of allegations of child sexual abuse. An Australian Royal Commission found that of 1,000

alleged cases investigated by Jehovah's Witness elders, not one was reported to the secular authorities. The Royal Commission also found that the Watchtower Society routinely provided false information to its elders. In 2021, however, Jehovah's Witnesses in Australia agreed to join the national Redress Scheme for sexual assault survivors, and in this way maintained its charitable status.

My own visit to the Kingdom Hall was intriguing, not least for the Bible Study. I've always welcomed their doorstep evangelism but their detailed beliefs I found more difficult, and as a physician I disagree with their ban on blood transfusions.

# 10. The Jews

*Jewish Synagogue*

Judaism is the foundation of the Christian faith and Jesus Christ was a Jew. Also, I am one-eighth Jewish which I thought was sufficient justification for me to attend a synagogue service. I love the Old Testament stories of a fearsome God who is best not messed with. At a Liberal synagogue on their Saturday Sabbath, I had a warm welcome and they loaned me a Yarmulke prayer cap and a prayer shawl. I joined the male

and female congregation sitting among each another, and during his address, the Rabbi had us in stitches with his stories. One was that his family had fallen out with Esau's family 2000 years ago, and they still hadn't made up. At the end of the service, they offered me salt and bread over a chat, and I enjoyed this enormously.

Judaism is the monotheistic religion of the Jewish people, with its roots in the Middle East during the Bronze Age. Modern Judaism evolved from Yahwism, which dates back to the 6th century BCE, and is an expression of the covenant that God established with the Israelites. Both Judaism and Islam trace their origins to the patriarch Abraham through his sons, Isaac and Ishmael, though Jews do not consider Jesus or Muhammad to be prophets.

Orthodox Judaism maintains that the Torah is divine in origin and should be strictly followed. Historically, special courts used to enforce these rules but today the practice is voluntary. In contrast, Reform Judaism says the rules are only guidelines and many Jews now classify themselves as secular, and largely ignore all organised religious life.

Jews are those born Jewish or converts to Judaism. In 2019, the world Jewish population was estimated at 14.7 million, about 45 % in Israel and 42 % in the United States and Canada, with most of the remainder in Europe. About six million Jews were

murdered in the Nazi holocaust of WWII.

The Torah is part of the Hebrew Bible and expands the original Five Books of Abraham. It strongly influenced later Abrahamic religions, including Christianity and Islam, and played a major role in modern civilisation. It is an account of the Israelite's relationship with God from their earliest history before the building of the Second Temple in 535 BCE. Abraham is hailed as the father of the Jewish people and as a reward for his act of faith in one God, he was promised that Isaac, his second son, would inherit the Land of Israel (Cana). Later, the descendants of Isaac's son Jacob were enslaved in Egypt, and God commanded Moses to lead their exodus home. At Mount Sinai, they received the five books of Moses and eventually God led them to the land of Israel where the tabernacle of the people was planted in the city of Shiloh. As time went on, the spiritual level of the nation declined to the point that God allowed the Philistines to capture the tabernacle. The people of Israel then told Samuel the prophet that they needed a permanent king, and Samuel appointed Saul to rule over them, and he was followed by David.

Once King David was established, he wanted to build a permanent temple, and as a reward for his actions, God promised David he would allow his son Solomon to build it. The Western Wall in Jerusalem is a remnant of the wall

encircling the Second Temple, and Temple Mount is the holiest site in Judaism. After Solomon's reign, the nation split into Israel in the north and Judah in the south. Israel was destroyed in 720 BCE, and Judah was conquered by Nebuchadnezzar in 586 BCE and exiled to Babylon. Later, many of them returned home, and after the conquest of Babylon by the Persians, a Second Temple was constructed and the old religious practices resumed.

During the Great Jewish Revolt in 66-73 CE, the Romans sacked Jerusalem and destroyed the Second Temple, forcibly removing all Jews from Judea. Many of the buildings in Rome, such as the Colosseum, were built with Jewish slave labour.

Scholars like Josephus and Maimonides have recorded Judaism's core tenets. In modern times, it lacks a centralised authority and there are many different variations of the basic beliefs. In addition to prayer services, traditional Jews recite prayers throughout the day, either when waking up in the morning, before eating or drinking, and after meals.

Traditional prayer clothes are commonplace. A kippah is the rounded brimless skullcap worn by many Jews while praying, eating, reciting blessings, or studying religious texts, worn at all times by some Jewish men. In size, they range from a small round cap that covers the back of the head to a large cap that covers the whole crown. Tzitzits are special knotted tassels

found on the four corners of tallit prayer shawls. A kittel is a white knee-length over garment worn by prayer leaders on High Holy days. It is traditional for the head of the household to wear a kittel at the Passover, and some bridegrooms wear one under their wedding canopy. Deceased Jewish males are often buried in a tallit and sometimes a kittel too.

There are numerous Jewish holidays, like Shabbat which commemorates God's day of rest after the six days of creation. The woman of the house welcomes Shabbat by lighting candles and reciting a blessing. The evening meal begins with the Kiddush, which is a blessing recited aloud over a cup of wine, and a mohtzi, which is a blessing recited over the bread. During Shabbat, Jews are forbidden to work, light fires, write letters, spend money, drive a car or use electricity.

At the festivals of Sukkot, Passover and Shavuot, it was customary to make pilgrimages to Jerusalem to offer sacrifices in the Temple.

Haggadah is a week-long holiday that commemorates the exodus from Egypt. Passover coincides with the barley harvest, where leavened products are removed from the house and homes are thoroughly cleaned to ensure no bread or bread by-products remain. Matzo is eaten instead of bread. Shavuot celebrates the revelation of the Torah to the Israelites on Mount Sinai. Its customs include eating dairy foods

(cheesecake and blintzes are special favourites), reading the Book of Ruth, decorating homes and synagogues with greenery, and wearing white clothing to symbolise purity. Sukkot commemorates the Israelites' forty years of wandering through the desert on their way to the Promised Land and is celebrated with the construction of temporary booths to represent the shelters the Israelites built during their wandering. It coincides with the fruit harvest and marks the end of the agricultural cycle. Sukkot concludes with Shemini Atzeret, where they pray for rain, and is celebrated with singing and dancing with the Torah scrolls. Rosh Hashanah is the Jewish New Year and marks the period of atonement leading up to Yom Kippur, during which Jews are commanded to search their souls and make amends for any sins committed. Holiday customs include blowing the shofar, or ram's horn in the synagogue, eating apples and honey, and saying blessings over symbolic foods, such as pomegranates. Yom Kippur or the Day of Atonement is the holiest day of the Jewish year, a day of communal fasting and praying for forgiveness for one's sins. Observant Jews spend the entire day in the synagogue, reciting prayers from a special prayerbook called a machzor. Even non-religious Jews make a point of attending synagogue services and fasting on Yom Kippur. On the eve before candles are lit, a pre-fast meal, the seudah mafseket, is eaten. It is

customary to wear white on Yom Kippur, and the following day, prayers are held from morning to evening. The final prayer service ends with a long blast of the shofar. Purim is a joyous Jewish holiday that commemorates the deliverance of the Persian Jews from an evil Haman who sought to exterminate them. It is characterised by recitations of the Book of Esther, gifts of food and drink, charity to the poor, and a celebratory meal. Other customs include drinking wine, eating pastries called hamantashen, dressing up in masks and costumes, and organising carnivals and parties. Hanukkah is observed in Jewish homes by the kindling of lights and marks the re-dedication of the Temple after its desecration by Antiochus Epiphanes. Hanukkah also commemorates the Miracle of the Oil when at the re-dedication of the Temple there was only enough consecrated oil to fuel the eternal flame for one day but it burned for the eight days it took to press new oil. Hanukkah is not mentioned in the Bible but has become widely celebrated in modern times because it falls at the time of Christmas and Divali. And finally, the Holy Day of Tisha B'Av commemorates the Holocaust and victims of terrorism.

Synagogues contain separate rooms for prayer, smaller ones for study, and an area for community use. There is no set blueprint for synagogues and the architectural shapes and interior designs vary greatly. The Reform movement mostly

refer to their synagogues as temples, and some traditional features include the ark where the Torah scrolls are kept behind an ornate curtain, an elevated platform with an eternal light in the pulpit where the prayer leader stands while praying. In addition to synagogues, other buildings of significance in Judaism include Yeshiva institutions of learning, and Mikvah ritual baths.

The Jewish dietary laws prepare food in accordance with what is termed 'kosher'. In order to be considered kosher, mammals must have split hooves and chew their cud (so not pigs), and for sea food, the animal must have fins and scales; certain types of seafood, such as shell fish, crustaceans and eels are therefore non-kosher. Concerning birds, a list of non-kosher species is given in the Torah. In addition, meat and poultry must come from a healthy animal slaughtered in a process known as shechita. Without the proper practices, a kosher animal is rendered non-kosher. The slaughtering process is intended to be quick and relatively painless to the animal. Forbidden parts of animals include the blood and some fats, and the area around the sciatic nerve. Halakha also forbids the consumption of meat and dairy products together. The use of certain dishes, serving utensils, and ovens may render food non-kosher, even utensils that have been previously used for non-kosher food. The Torah does not give

reasons for most of these laws. However, a number of explanations have been offered, including ritual purity, impulse control, obedience to God, improving health, reducing cruelty to animals and preserving community distinctness. The non-consumption of the blood of animals is because Jews believe this is where their souls are contained.

Another important ritual of purity law relates to the segregation of menstruating women, though these are not followed by Liberal Jews. For example, the Torah mandates that a woman in her menstrual period must abstain from sexual relationships for seven days and Rabbinical law forbids the husband from touching or sharing a bed with his wife during this time. Afterwards, her purification requires a ritual bath. In addition, Ethiopian Jews keep menstruating women in separate huts and do not allow them into their temples.

Other rites of passage in a Jew's life include welcoming male babies into the covenant through circumcision on their eighth day of life. The baby boy is also given his Hebrew name in the ceremony. The Bar Mitzvah is the passage from childhood to adulthood and takes place when a female Jew is 12 and a male Jew is 13 years old. Weddings take place under a chuppah wedding canopy, which symbolises a happy house. At the end of the ceremony, the groom breaks a glass with his foot, symbolising continued mourning for the destruction of the

Temple, and the diaspora of the Jewish people.

The priesthood is an inherited position, and although priests now only have ceremonial duties, they are still honoured in Jewish communities. The professional clergy in a synagogue includes the Rabbi who are charged with answering the legal questions of a congregation, and the Hazzan who are trained vocalists with knowledge of traditional tunes, and understanding of their meaning. The shaliach tzibur, or shatz, lead those assembled in prayer and sometimes pray on their behalf. In Orthodox congregations, only men can be prayer leaders, but progressive communities allow women to serve this role. The baal keriah recites the weekly Torah reading. Many congregations, especially larger ones, also rely on a gabbai who calls people up to the Torah and makes certain that the synagogue is kept clean and well supplied. The dayan is an ordained rabbi with special legal training to handle marriage and divorce cases, and conversion and financial disputes. The Mohel is an expert in the laws of circumcision and also performs them. In order for meat to be kosher, it must be slaughtered by a shochet who is an expert in the laws of Kashrut. In addition, the Torah scrolls and other official bills must be written by a sofer who is an expert in Hebrew calligraphy. Finally, the yeshiva is a scholar responsible for ensuring attendance and proper conduct, who gives lectures on

Jewish ethics. And the mashgiach supervises the kosher manufacturers, importers, caterers and restaurants.

Around the 1st century BCE, there were Jewish sects like the Pharisees, Sadducees, Zealots and Essenes, but after the destruction of the Second Temple these vanished. Christianity survived, and became a new religion. Others like the Amalekites survived with traditions of their own. Over a long time, Jews formed distinct ethnic groups in different geographic areas, like the Ashkenazi of Central and Eastern Europe, and the Sephardi of Spain, Portugal and North Africa. These too developed differences in their prayers and traditions.

Antisemitism arose during the Middle Ages in the form of persecutions, pogroms, forced conversions, expulsions, social restrictions and ghettos. With the rise of Christianity, the main motive for such attacks was the Christian blame for Christ's crucifixion by the Jews. In contrast, Jewish people who lived under Muslim rule experienced tolerance and integration.

In the late 18th century Enlightenment, increasing numbers of Jews assimilated into Christian Europe. In Europe and the United States, Reform Judaism relaxed the legal obligations limiting Jewish relations with non-Jews. There were also massive movements of Jews following the Holocaust and the creation of the state of Israel.

Christianity was originally a sect of Second Temple Judaism

but the two religions diverged in the first century. The differences between Christianity and Judaism originally centred on whether Jesus was the Jewish Messiah, but eventually they became irreconcilable.

Jews in Christian lands were subject to humiliating legal restrictions. These included the provisions requiring Jews to wear specific clothing such as the Jewish hats and yellow badges, restricting them to certain cities, towns or ghettos, and forbidding them from certain trades, for example, selling new clothes. There were also special taxes levied on Jews, exclusion from public life, restraints on religious ceremonies, and the linguistic censorship of Hebrew and Yiddish. Some countries went even further and completely expelled Jews, as was the case in England in 1290. The first Jewish settlers in North America arrived in the Dutch colony of New Amsterdam in 1654 but were forbidden to hold public office, open retail shops, or establish synagogues, and when the colony was seized by the British in 1664, these restrictions remained.

I find all this fascinating. I know it sounds like a cliché but some of my best friends are Jews. I liked the synagogue service a lot and writing this reminds me that I promised them I would go again.

# 11. The Mormons

*Mormons Trekking West to Utah*

I became aware of the Mormons when I visited a temple in California and I was grateful when they helped me research some family ancestry. Also, when I came back to the UK, a group of them turned up on my door step to enquire after me and my family which further impressed me.

The Mormons are the principal branch of the Latter Day Saints movement, started by Joseph Smith in New York during the 1830s. It began with his publication of the Book of

Mormon which he claimed was a translation of golden plates inscribed with the religious history of an ancient American civilisation, and which the prophet-historian Mormon compiled. Smith claimed that an angel directed him to the spot where the plates were buried on Cumorah Hill in Palmyra, New York.

Mormons self-identify as Christian, but many consider them non-Christian because some of their beliefs differ from the Nicene Creed. They believe that Christ's church was restored through Joseph Smith and is guided by living prophets and apostles. Mormons believe in the Bible and the Book of Mormon, and that all people are the spirit children of God. The centre of the Mormon culture is in Utah, and North America has more Mormons than any other continent. In 2020, the LDS Church reported 16,663,663 members worldwide.

From the start, Mormons tried to establish what they call Zion, a utopian society of the righteous. Smith attempted to build Zion in Utah where converts could gather together in Mormon villages. In modern times, Zion is still an ideal, though Mormons now gather in separate congregations rather than centrally.

The early church spread westward as Smith sent missionaries to preach the new faith, but in 1838, tensions with Missouri settlers escalated into the Mormon War. The

governor of Missouri ordered the Mormons driven out from the state and some 8,000 migrated east into Illinois. In 1839, they purchased the town of Commerce, drained swamp land on the banks of the Mississippi River, and constructed their Nauvoo Temple. The town became their new gathering place, and it grew rapidly, with converts immigrating from Europe.

Meanwhile, Smith introduced temple ceremonies to bind families more tightly together, and new doctrines such as plural marriage. He created a service organisation for women called the Relief Society and published the story of his First Vision when he was 14 years old, in which the Father and the Son appeared to him. This was regarded by some Mormons as the most important event in human history after the birth and resurrection of Jesus Christ.

One of his central doctrines was the practice of plural marriage. But in 1844, local opposition to this escalated into conflict with the other residents of Illinois and Missouri. Smith was arrested, and he and his brother Hyrum were killed by a mob in Carthage, Illinois. Their deaths caused a succession crisis and Brigham Young assumed the leadership of the main group. By 1852, up to 30 percent of Mormon families were entering plural marriages as a religious duty. The practice made economic sense as many plural wives were single women who arrived alone in Utah and needed the support of a husband.

But in 1857, more tensions over polygamy escalated between Mormons and other Americans. In 1878, the US Supreme Court ruled that religious duty was not a legal defence for polygamy. Many Mormon polygamists went into hiding as Congress seized their church assets. As a result, in 1890 Mormon president Wilford Woodruff suspended the practice and in 1904 banned it. Eventually, the church adopted a policy of excommunicating members who practised polygamy, and relations with the US government improved. But about 20,000 broke away from the LDS Church and became fundamentalist Mormons.

Mormons dedicate significant time and resources to serving their church and many proselytise full-time. They forbid alcoholic beverages, tobacco, tea, coffee, and addictive substances. They are very family-oriented and have strong connections across the generations and through extended families. They believe that families can be sealed together beyond death. As a result, many hold weekly family home evenings for bonding, study, prayer and other activities.

They also have a strict law of chastity, requiring abstention from sexual relations outside marriage, and fidelity within marriage. LGBT Mormons remain in good standing in the church if they abstain from homosexual relations and obey the law of chastity but only about ten percent of homosexuals stay

within the church.

Two years after Joseph Smith's death, conflicts again escalated between Mormons and other Illinois residents. To prevent another war, Brigham Young led the **Mormon Pioneers to tempor**ary winter quarters in Nebraska and then on to what became the Utah Territory. Having failed to build Zion within the confines of American society, the Mormons began to construct a society in isolation, based on their beliefs and values. The cooperative ethic that Mormons had developed became important as settlers branched out and colonised a large desert region known as the Mormon corridor. Colonising efforts were seen as religious duties, and the new villages were governed by lay religious leaders called Mormon Bishops. The Mormons viewed land as a commonwealth, and they devised and maintained cooperative systems like irrigation that allowed them to build a farming community in the desert.

From 1849 to 1852, the Mormons established missions in Europe, Latin America and the South Pacific. Converts were expected to come to Zion, and over 70,000 immigrated to America; many came from England and Scandinavia, and were quickly assimilated into the Mormon community. Many of these crossed the Great Plains in wagons drawn by oxen, while some later groups pulled their possessions in handcarts. Then, during the 1860s, newcomers began using the rail roads.

But in 1857, tensions again escalated over polygamy and the theocratic rule of Brigham Young. In 1857, US President James Buchanan sent an army to Utah, and, fearing a repeat of Missouri and Illinois, the Mormons determined to torch their homes if they were invaded. A relatively peaceful Utah War ensued, the most notable violence being the Mountain Meadows massacre in which leaders of a local Mormon militia ordered the killing of a civilian emigrant party travelling through Utah. Young was forced to step down from his position as governor and was replaced by a non-Mormon called Alfred Cumming.

Mormons began to reintegrate into the American mainstream. In 1929, the Mormon Tabernacle Choir started broadcasting on national radio. In the 1930s, Mormons began migrating out of Utah because of the Great Depression. As they spread out, church leaders had to create programs to preserve their tight-knit communities. In addition to weekly church services, Mormons began participating in programs such as boy scouting, young women's groups, church-sponsored dances, ward basketball, camping trips, plays and religious education programmes for college students. During the Great Depression, the church started a welfare programme to meet the needs of poor members, which has since grown to include a humanitarian branch that now provides relief to

disaster victims.

The 1960s and 1970s brought changes such as women's liberation and civil rights and Mormon leaders became alarmed by the sexual revolution, recreational drugs and moral relativism. As a result, Mormons today are probably less integrated in mainstream society than they were in the 1960s.

Although Black people were always members of Mormon congregations, their numbers were small. From 1852 to 1978, the LDS Church restricted black African men from being ordained to the priesthood. The church was sharply criticised for this during the civil rights movement, but the ban remained in force until 1978. In general, Mormons welcomed the change and since 1978, Black membership has grown to approximately 500,000 members (about five percent of the total membership). A Genesis Group was formed specifically for Black members.

Same-sex marriages are not performed or supported by the LDS Church. Members are encouraged to marry and have children, and LDS families tend to be larger than average. Mormons are opposed to abortion, except when pregnancy is the result of incest or rape, or when the life or health of the mother is in serious jeopardy.

Many adult Mormons wear religious undergarments and dress modestly. Tattoos and body piercings are discouraged,

with the exception of a single pair of earrings for women.

Nowadays, many LDS Church members do not participate in church services and only 30 percent attend worship. Disengagement occurs most frequently between the ages of 16 and 25, but the Church maintains that most return in later life. Liberal Mormons look to scripture for spiritual guidance, but may not believe the teachings are literally true.

Mormons believe in a pre-mortal existence, where people were the spirit children of God and their bodies were received on earth to be tested and learn to progress to full joy. The most important part of the plan involved Jesus coming to earth as the Son of God to conquer sin and death so that God's other children could return as well. According to Mormons, every person who lives on earth will be resurrected, and nearly all will be received into various kingdoms of glory.

According to Mormons, a deviation from the original principles of Christianity began not long after the ascension of Jesus Christ, marked by the corruption of Christian doctrine by Greek and other philosophies. Mormons believe that God restored the early Christian Church through Joseph Smith, that angels appeared to him and bestowed priestly authority upon him.

Mormons believe their church is the only true and living church because of the divine authority restored through Smith

but other religions have elements of the truth and are of some value.

# 12. The Bahá'ís

*Universal House of Justice, Haifa*

I found the Bahá'ís on the internet and when I attended a service, it turned out to be a meeting in the home of one of the lead members. There were about 30 present, including white Protestants, Asian Muslims and Hindus, some Jews and some with no faith. It was very friendly and we all stood chatting for an hour with a cup of tea and some biscuits. The theme we talked about was the importance of friendship and tolerance

across all religious faiths, and only at the end did we close our eyes and say a short non-denominational prayer which was addressed to God, but with no mention of Jesus Christ, Mohammad or the Buddha. And when it was over, we all offered to help wash up the cups but were graciously turned away and were shown to the door to find our parked cars.

The Bahá'í faith was founded in the 19th century and teaches the essential worth of all religions and the unity of all people. Established by Baha Ullah, it began in Iran where it faced persecution from the outset. It now has between five and eight million adherents and is spread throughout most countries. The faith has three central figures: the Bab (1819-1850), who is considered a herald who taught his followers that God would send a prophet similar to Jesus or Mohammad and who was executed by Iranian authorities in 1850; Bahá'u'lláh (1817-1892), who claimed to be that prophet and who faced exile and lifelong imprisonment; and his son Abdu'l-Bahá (1844-1921), who was released from confinement and made teaching trips to Europe and the United States. After Abdu'l-Bahá's death in 1921, the leadership fell to his grandson, Shogi Effendi (1897-1957).

Bahá'ís annually elect local, regional and national Spiritual Assemblies who govern the religion's affairs, and every five years an election is held for the Universal House of Justice,

which is the nine-member supreme governing institution in Haifa, Israel, situated near the Shrine of Bab.

According to Bahá'í teachings, religion has been revealed in an orderly and progressive way by a single God through the world religious leaders like Buddha, Jesus and Mohammad, and more recently by Báb and Bahá'u'lláh. Bahá'ís regard the world's major religions as fundamentally unified in purpose, though diverging in social practices and interpretations. The Bahá'í faith stresses the unity of all people, and the goal of a unified world order that ensures the prosperity of all nations, races, creeds and classes. Letters which were written by Bahá'u'lláh have been collected and assembled into a canon of Bahai scriptures called the Kitáb-i-Íqán, Some Unanswered Questions and the Dawn Breakers.

Bahá'ís believe that God reveals his will through divine messengers, whose purpose is to transform the character of humankind and develop moral and spiritual qualities. Religion is thus seen as orderly, unified, and progressive from age to age.

The Bahá'í writings describe a single, personal, inaccessible, omniscient, omnipresent, imperishable and almighty God who is the creator of all things in the universe. The existence of God and the universe is thought to be eternal, without a beginning or end. Though inaccessible directly, God is seen as conscious of creation, with a will and purpose expressed

through messengers called Manifestations.

Bahá'í teachings state that God is too great for humans to fully comprehend by themselves. Therefore, human understanding of God is achieved through his revelations via his Manifestations.

The Bahá'í writings state that human beings have a rational soul, and that this provides the species with a unique capacity to recognize God's status and humanity's relationship with its creator. Every human is seen to have a duty to recognise God through his messengers and conform to their teachings. Through recognition and obedience, service to humanity and regular prayer and spiritual practice, the Bahá'í writings state that the soul becomes closer to God, the spiritual ideal in Bahá'í belief. According to Bahá'í belief, when a human dies, the soul is permanently separated from the body and carries on in the next world where it is judged by the person's actions in the physical world. Heaven and Hell are taught to be spiritual states of nearness or distance from God that describe relationships in this world and the next, and not physical places of reward and punishment achieved after death.

The Bahá'í writings emphasise the essential equality of human beings and the abolition of prejudice. Humanity is seen as essentially one, though highly varied; its diversity of race and culture are seen as worthy of appreciation and acceptance.

Doctrines of racism, nationalism, caste, social class and gender-based hierarchy are seen as artificial impediments to unity. The teachings also state that the unification of humanity is the paramount issue in the religious and political conditions of the present world.

Another outgrowth of the concept is the need for a united world federation, and some practical recommendations to encourage its realisation involve the establishment of a universal language, a standard economy and system of measurement, universal compulsory education, and an international court of arbitration to settle disputes between nations. Nationalism, according to this viewpoint, should be abandoned in favour of allegiance to the whole of mankind. With regard to the pursuit of world peace, Bahá'u'lláh prescribed a world-embracing collective security arrangement.

The writings of the Báb and Bahá'u'lláh are considered as divine revelation, the writings of Abdu'l-Bahá and Shogi Effendi as their authoritative interpretation, and those of the Universal House of Justice as their authoritative elucidation. Some measure of divine guidance is assumed for all of these texts.

In this vein, in the 1970s the Rubi Institute was founded by Bahais in Colombia to offer courses on Bahá'í beliefs. The associated Ruhi Foundation, whose purpose was to consolidate

new Bahá'ís, was registered in 1992, and since the late 1990s the courses of the Ruhi Institute have been dominant in teaching the Bahá'í Faith around the world. By 2013, there were over 300 Bahá'í training institutes around the world and 100,000 people participating in courses. Annually the Universal House of Justice sends a message to the worldwide community updating current developments and guidance for the year to come. Any male Bahá'í, 21 years or older, is eligible to be elected to the Universal House of Justice; all other positions are open to male and female Bahá'ís. The following are a few examples from Bahá'u'lláh's teachings on personal conduct that are required or encouraged of his followers:

Bahá'ís over the age of 15 should recite an obligatory prayer each day, using fixed words and form. In addition to the daily obligatory prayer, Bahá'ís should offer a daily devotional prayer and meditate and study the sacred scripture. Adult Bahá'ís should observe a nineteen day fast each year during daylight hours in March. There are specific requirements for Bahá'í burial that include a specified prayer to be read at the interment. Embalming or cremating the body is strongly discouraged. Bahá'ís should make a 19% voluntary payment on any wealth in excess of what is necessary to live comfortably, after the remittance of any outstanding debt: the payments go

to the Universal House of Justice. Back-biting and gossip are prohibited, and drinking or selling alcohol is forbidden. Sexual intercourse is only permitted between a husband and wife, and premarital, extramarital or homosexual intercourse are forbidden. Participation in partisan politics is forbidden and begging as a profession is forbidden.

Bahá'ís intending to marry are asked to obtain a thorough understanding of the other's character before deciding to marry. Although parents should not choose partners for their children, once two individuals decide to marry, they must receive the consent of their living biological parents, whether they are Bahá'í or not. The Bahá'í marriage ceremony is simple; the only compulsory part of the wedding is the reading of the wedding vows prescribed by Bahá'u'lláh which both the groom and the bride read in the presence of two witnesses. Transgender people can gain gender recognition if they have medically transitioned and undergone sex surgery. After this, they are considered transitioned and may be married.

The Bihá'í year consists of 19 months, each having 19 days, with four or five intercalary days to make a full solar year. The Bahá'í New Year corresponds to the traditional Iranian New Year, called Naw-Ruz, and occurs on the Venal Equinox.

Once every Bahá'í month there is a gathering of the Bahá'í community called a Nineteen Day Feast with three parts: first,

a devotional prayer and reading from Bahá'í scripture; second, an administrative part for consultation and community matters; and third, a social part for the community to interact freely.

The Bihá'í week days and each of their 19 months are named after an attribute of God, like Baha, IIm and Jamal. And Bahá'ís have 11 holy days when work is suspended so as to commemorate the history of the religion.

In the face of Iranian suppression of women's rights, the Bihá'í faith gave greater freedom to women, and created schools, agricultural co-ops and clinics. Worldwide in 1979, there were 129 Bahá'í socio-economic development projects and by 1987 this number had increased to 1482 under the direction of their Universal House of Justice in Haifa, Israel.

Bahá'ís have strongly supported world government and organisations like the League of Nations and the United Nations.

In 1979, Iranian Bahá'ís had their homes ransacked and they were banned from attending university and holding government jobs. Several hundred were gaoled.

# 13. The Quakers

*A Pennsylvania Quaker*

At the Society of Friends service I attended, thirty or so Quakers sat in a silent circle and listened to the wind in the rafters and

the rain beating against the windows. After about 20 minutes, one of them stood up and said he wished to tell us some thoughts he had had that week. He proceeded to relate how a Quaker called Norman Morrison set fire to himself beneath the Pentagon office of the US Secretary of State for Defence in protest against the Vietnam War. He carried his baby daughter in his arms and the crowd shouted, "Throw the child, save the child." He did and she survives to this day. Following this, another Quaker called Richard Nixon withdrew the American troops from Vietnam and ended the conflict.

Then we all fell silent again and I liked it so much that next time I was in the Lake District, I visited George Fox's home at Swarthmoor, where he founded the Quaker movement.

The Quakers have a celebrated history, and founded Greenpeace, CND, Amnesty International and Oxfam. Famous Quakers include George Fox, William Penn, Elizabeth Fry, and the Cadbury family. Quakerism arose in 17th-century England among those groups breaking from the Church of England. They sought to convert others by travelling throughout the world and preaching the Gospel.

They stressed a relationship with God through Jesus Christ and a belief in the universal brotherhood of believers. Their personal experience was acquired by studying the Bible, and they focused their private lives on the goal of Christian

perfection.

Quakers use 'thee' as a non-gender pronoun, refuse to participate in war, wear plain clothes, refuse to swear oaths, oppose slavery and are teetotal. Because they were refused entry into the professions, some founded banks like Barclays and Lloyds, food manufacturers like Cadbury's, Rowntrees and Fry's, and companies like Clarks Shoes. They led efforts for the abolition of slavery and prison reform, and some were awarded the Nobel Peace Prize.

After the English Civil War of 1642-1651, a young man called George Fox had a revelation and became convinced it was possible to have a direct experience of Christ without the intervention of ordained clergy. He travelled around England, the Netherlands and the Caribbean, seeking to convert new adherents to his faith. He considered himself to be restoring the original, true Christian church. But in 1650, he was brought before magistrates Gervaise Bennett and Nathaniel Barton on a charge of blasphemy. Bennett called Fox's followers Quakers because Fox bade them to tremble at the word of God.

The number of Quakers had increased to 60,000 in England by 1680 but the dominant Protestant view was that they were a blasphemous challenge to social and political order, which led to their persecution under the Quaker Acts of 1662 and 1664.

Together with Margaret Fell, the wife of Thomas Fell, the vice-chancellor of the Duchy of Lancaster and an eminent judge, Fox developed new concepts of family and community that emphasised piety, faith and love. With the restructuring of the family came new roles for women, with Fox and Fell viewing the family mother as essential to her children and to her husband. Eventually, Quaker women became involved in the wider community.

The persecution of Quakers in North America began in 1656 when English Quaker missionaries Mary Fisher and Ann Austin began preaching in Boston and were considered heretics. They were imprisoned and banished by the Massachusetts Bay Colony, their books were burned, and their property was confiscated. They were then imprisoned in severe conditions, and finally deported. In 1660, an English Quaker, Mary Dyer, was hanged on Boston Common for defying a Puritan ban on Quakers. She was one of the four executed Quakers known as the 'Boston martyrs'. Then in 1661, King Charles II forbad Massachusetts to execute Quakers and three years later he sent a royal governor and signed a parliamentary Toleration Act.

Some Quakers, or the Religious Society of Friends (Friends), migrated to the north-eastern United States in the 1660s in search of a more tolerant environment and in 1665 in

Shrewsbury, New Jersey, they built a meeting house which was visited by George Fox from England. They established thriving communities in the Delaware Valley, Rhode Island and Pennsylvania and in the next 100 years, 36 state governors were Quakers. West Jersey and Pennsylvania were established by William Penn in 1676, and run as an American commonwealth under Quaker principles. Penn signed a peace treaty with Tammany, the leader of the Delaware native Americans. Early Quakers established more communities and meeting houses in North Carolina and Maryland. It was Quakers who introduced democracy to the Pennsylvania legislature, the US Bill of Rights, the US Constitution, trial by jury, equal rights for men and women, and public education, and the Liberty Bell was cast by Quakers in Philadelphia.

Early Quakers tolerated behaviour that challenged conventional etiquette, but during the 18th century, they became more inward-looking and less active in converting others. The Religious Society of Friends dates from this period, this formal name being derived from the Friends of Light and Truth.

Around the time of the American revolutionary war, some American Quakers left the main Society over support for the war, and in the 19th century there were further splits between rural, poor and wealthy urban groups.

But when Elias Hicks left in 1827, Quakers in Britain refused to correspond with him. Then Isaac Crewdson in England resigned, along with 48 fellow members of the Manchester Meeting House, and 250 of them eventually joined the Plymouth Brethren.

Orthodox Friends became more evangelical during the 19th century, and a Second Great Awakening was led by Joseph Gurney. From the 1870s it became common to have home mission meetings on Sunday evenings and Friends in Great Britain started missionary activities in India, Madagascar, China, Kenya, Uganda, Rwanda and Ceylon.

The new Charles Darwin theory of evolution was opposed by many Quakers, but some of the younger ones supported it and cited the doctrine of progressive revelation. In the United States, Joseph Moore taught the theory of evolution at Earlham College as early as 1861 but creationism still dominated Quakers in other parts. During WWI and WWII, Friends' opposition to war was put to the test. Many became conscientious objectors and some formed the Non-Combatants Corps and the Friends' Ambulance Service.

From the beginning, Quaker women like Margaret Fell played an important role. However, some resented this. George Fox faced resistance to establishing women's meetings. Birmingham Quaker, John Cadbury, founded Cadbury Ltd in

1824, selling tea, coffee and drinking chocolate. Abraham Darby and Edward Pease played an important role in ironmaking and building the Stockton and Darlington Railway, the world's first public railway to use steam locomotives. Other industries with prominent Quaker businesses included Lloyds and Barclays Banking Groups, Allen and Hanbury's Pharmaceuticals, Fry's Chocolate, Rowntree's confectionary and Huntley and Palmer's biscuits.

In England, Quaker schools sprang up with the Friends' School Saffron Walden being the most prominent. Edith Pye established a national Famine Relief Committee in 1942, and a network of local committees, the most energetic of which was the Oxford Committee for Famine Relief, which became Oxfam. In 1971, Dorothy Stowe founded Greenpeace.

In early colonial America, it was common for Quakers to own slaves, but during the 1700s, disquiet resulted in an abolition movement. Nine of the twelve founding members of The Society for the Abolition of the Slave Trade were Quakers, and in England, six Friends presented a petition to Parliament against slavery. But Quakers could not serve as Members of Parliament, and they had to rely on the help of Anglicans like William Wilberforce and James Stephen. In 1790, the Society of Friends petitioned the US Congress to abolish slavery. Levi Coffin and Isaac Hopper played a major role in helping

enslaved people escape north through a secret route known as the Underground Railroad.

I liked the Quakers a great deal and enjoyed the meeting I attended, so I promised them I would go again and I have done.

# 14. The Salvation Army

*A Salvation Army Brass Band*

Most people love the Salvation Army and especially their brass bands which come on to the streets in all winds and weathers to entertain the public at Christmas, raising funds for the most down-trodden in society. At my local Salvation Army citadel, I was told their band usually accompanied the hymn singing, but many of their players had flu and could not play that day. At the end of the service, I asked them if I could help prepare and serve a hot Christmas Day lunch for homeless people. I

was told yes, but the waiting list was long and they always had too many volunteers for this, so I am still waiting for their call.

The Salvation Army grew out of Methodism, and its distinctive character is its use of military titles. Their ministers can be recognised by the colour-coded epaulettes on their uniform dress shirts and in Scotland there is a Salvation Army tartan. The officer ranks are Lieutenant, Captain, Major, Colonel, Commissioner and General. Promotion depends mainly on years of service, and officers are reassigned to different posts every two to five years, when they are sometimes moved great distances. Their flag is a symbol of the Army's war against social evils, the red symbolising the blood of Jesus Christ, the yellow the fire of the Holy Spirit and the blue the purity of God the Father. They have a salute which involves raising the right hand above shoulder-height, with the index finger pointing upwards, which signifies recognition of a fellow citizen of heaven and a pledge to help others get to heaven.

When saluting in response to applause, it also signifies that Salvationists wish to give any glory to God and not to themselves. In some instances, the salute is accompanied with a shout of 'Hallelujah!'

The Salvation Army was founded as the East London Christian Mission in 1865 by the Methodist preacher William

Booth and his wife, Catherine. Its first meeting was in the Blind Beggar Tavern, later made infamous by the Kray twins. Later on, when the Salvation Army preached against alcohol, its meetings were disrupted by crowds who threw stones and bottles, riots that were organised by the pub owners and brewers who stood to lose out from teetotalism.

In 1878, Booth introduced the Army's military structure and became its first General. His early motivation was to convert prostitutes, gamblers and alcoholics to Christianity using the three Ss: first soup, then soap, and finally salvation. Catherine on the other hand was the one to solicit wealthy people to gain support for their work. She also acted as a religious minister, and the Foundation Deed of the Christian Mission stated that women had the same rights as men. It permitted the ordination of women, and whilst officers were only allowed to marry other officers, this rule was later relaxed. Husbands and wives share the same rank and are given joint assignments.

The Salvation Army campaigned in New Zealand against the Homosexual Reform Act 1986, and in San Francisco in 1997 it declined a government grant of $3.5million to promote equal rights for homosexuals. In 2000, in the United Kingdom opposed the repeal of a Local Government Act which prevented local authorities from promoting homosexuality,

and as of 2001, the organisation does not marry homosexuals or appoint them as ministers. But it does stand against homophobia which victimises gay people and can reinforce feelings of alienation, loneliness and despair.

The current international leader elected by its High Council is General Brian Peddle and its operating costs in 2004 were $2.6 billion, enabling it to help more than 32 million people in the US alone. It runs disaster relief in refugee camps across the world, and especially among displaced people in Africa.

Their buildings are citadels and they often combine thrift stores or charity shops, referred to as the 'Sally Ann', to raise money by selling used clothing, housewares and toys. The shops in the United Kingdom participate in the government's Work Force programme where benefit claimants work for no wages for 20 to 40 hours per week. Articles not sold are recycled and turned into other items such as carpet underlay.

The Salvation Army also helps ex-felons – they believe in giving people a second chance. Job opportunities are nationwide and felons are able to move up to become managers in the corporate offices, and from early on they are trusted with money.

Some shops are associated with an Adult Rehabilitation Centre where men and women make a six-month commitment to live and work. They are unpaid but are provided with board

and lodging. Most in ARCs are men and the programs are usually designed to combat drug and alcohol addiction.

Farmland at Hadleigh in Essex was acquired in 1891 to provide training for men referred from Salvation Army shelters. It featured market gardens, orchards and brickfields. More than 60% of its participants find permanent employment. The Salvation Army also operates children's summer camps, adult day care centres, homeless hostels, addiction dependency programs, children's and elderly care homes, mother and baby centres, women's and men's refuges, hospitals, schools, after-school programs, food pantries, and elderly overnight warming stations.

In 1885, an escapee from a brothel arrived at the door of the Salvation Army and sought help, following which Catherine Booth wrote to Queen Victoria seeking support for a Parliamentary Bill to protect girls. The Salvation Army organised a petition of 340,000 signatures which was deposited in the House of Commons by eight uniformed Salvationists. There were mass meetings and an investigation into child prostitution. The *Pall Mall Gazette* launched a campaign called the Maiden Tribute of Modern Babylon to expose the extent of child prostitution, and gave the example of a girl called Eliza who was procured for £5. She was cared for and eventually testified as a key witness in the trial of the prostitute

who had arranged her sale. Safeguarding legislation in a new Act of Parliament then made provision for the protection of girls and the suppression of brothels.

The Salvation Army does not perform baptism or Holy Communion but its officers conduct marriages, and the 'mercy seat' in the citadels is available for anyone to kneel in prayer.

There is no requirement for anyone attending services to be a member of the Salvation Army, and they are like many other denominations with hymns and scripture readings, and Sunday Schools. They sing hymns from the official *Songbook of the Salvation Army*, and the music is often accompanied by a brass band. In addition, there are financial collections called Tithes and Offerings, and the services conclude with a benediction.

The Soldier's Covenant was formerly known as the Articles of War which is the creed of the Salvation Army. Every person has to sign it to become a Soldier of Christ. Positional Statements describe the Salvation Army policy on social and moral issues, and are formulated by their International Moral and Social Council. The Salvation Army opposes euthanasia, assisted suicide, abortion, capital punishment, racism, slavery and human trafficking.

Their Family Tracing Service was established in 1885, and thousands of people are traced every year on behalf of their relatives. The Salvation Army includes various youth groups,

and its sponsored Scout and Guide packs allow anyone to join. Some citadels have Salvation Army Guards and Legions' Associations. Its youth groups for girls are known as Girl Guards for the older girls, and Sunbeams for the younger ones. In the 21st century, the Salvation Army of the United Kingdom created a youth branch called Alove, the Salvation Army for a new generation and a member of the National Council for Voluntary Youth Services.

In 1880, it started its work in other countries. When George Scott Railton and his team arrived in the USA, they started work in Harry Hill's Variety Theatre. Their first notable convert was Ash Barrel Jimmie who had so many convictions for drunkenness, the judge sentenced him to attend the Salvation Army. The New York corps was founded as a result of Jimmy's rehabilitation. The Salvation Army's reputation in the United States rose as a result of its disaster relief efforts following the Galveston Hurricane and the San Francisco earthquake.

The newly founded Salvation Army in Japan encountered child prostitution, which resulted from the system of Debt Bondage. After they sought an Imperial ordinance for girls' freedom, a pioneer Salvationist called Gunpei Yamamuro and his wife Kieko took charge of a home for girls wanting to give up prostitution. In 1900, another ordinance ruled that women

who wished to give up prostitution only had to go to the nearest police station for help.

The Salvation Army headquarters are in London and worldwide there are over 1.7 million Salvationists. There are adherents who do not commit to be a soldier but who attend the Salvation Army as their church. An International Congress of the Salvation Army is normally held every ten years and it now operates in 133 countries. It was one of the first relief agencies on the scene of the September 11 attacks in New York City in 2001, and provided prayer support for the families of missing people. Today in the US, over 25,000 bell ringers with red kettles are stationed near retail stores to fundraise during the weeks before Christmas. In WWI, over 250 Salvation Army volunteers went overseas to France to provide supplies and baked goods for American soldiers. The women who served doughnuts to the troops fried them in soldiers' helmets and were known as Doughnut Lassies; it was they who popularised doughnuts in the United States.

William Booth's dying wish was for the Salvation Army to be established in China and this was fulfilled in 1912 by Bramwell Booth, his son. In 1915, the first officers were sent there during the 1931 famine and fed 100,000 people daily. But following political difficulties in 1952, the Army withdrew from the mainland though it continued in Macau, Hong Kong

and Taiwan.

As the popularity of the early organisation grew and Salvationists worked their way through the streets of London attempting to convert individuals, they were sometimes confronted with unruly crowds. The Fry family from Wiltshire began playing music to distract the crowds. In 1891, a Salvation Army band attempted to parade and play music in Eastbourne, Sussex. This was in contravention of local by-laws and resulted in the arrest of nine Salvationists. Unperturbed, the Army continued to parade in defiance of the law, and gathered support for a change in legislation. Over the next few months, the situation escalated and there were riots to which mounted police were called to maintain order. The tradition of having musicians flourished and eventually grew into the brass bands that we see today. Across the world, the brass band has become the symbol of Salvationists. Their choirs are called Songster Brigades and their premier Brigade is the International Staff Songsters. The Army's Joy Strings were a UK pop group in the 1960s, reaching the popular music charts and featuring on national television. And there were other popular bands around the world like The Imsidez, Moped, Agent C, and Electralyte. Saytunes is an internet website to encourage and promote contemporary Salvation Army bands. Another musical feature of the Salvation Army is its tambourines, their

colourful ribbons representing the colours of the Salvation Army flag, mainly played by women. In many countries, the Salvation Army is recognised during the Christmas season with its volunteers and employees who stand outside shops and play Christmas carols, or ring bells to inspire passers-by to place donations in red kettles, a tradition that developed whereby gold coins or bundles of money bills are included.

# 15. The Bruderhof

*Two Bruderhof women taking their child to school*

The Bruderhof are a community who live in their own closed villages but invite guests to stay with them. I went to stay for a week as a guest in the home of the man, who repaired their musical instruments, and his wife, who helped organise the communal kitchens. This was wonderful hospitality and to pay for my upkeep I went to work in their wooden toy factory, alongside companions from France, Germany, Austria and the United States. All the members took turns to prepare and serve

the communal meals. At my first meal, they introduced me to the community and everyone clapped a welcome. Then, as the food was served, someone struck up a hymn and everyone joined in until it was time for the grace and for the meal to start. It was all quite wonderful.

Everyone in the village contributed as best they could to the communal life, whether teaching in the community school, nursing the elderly and the sick, or working the community farm where they grew crops and raised animals. I had a room to myself, and in the factory I helped make children's toys alongside a German called Rudiger. I attended a wedding and the whole village turned out to wish the young couple every happiness, after which we all enjoyed a simple reception.

They told me their teenagers are encouraged to leave the village and stay in London for a year, at a hostel they run for that purpose. Only when they have experienced the outside world with its luxuries and distractions are they asked to decide what to do with their lives, and nearly all of them return home.

Finally, the village welcomed back a group who had gone to Austria to help set up a new community and spread the message about their way of life. When the time came for me to leave, I felt this was a good way to live and I asked if I could visit them again. I was told that many visitors feel the same way, including Rowan Williams, the former Archbishop of

Canterbury.

The Bruderhof are Anabaptists, like the Amish and the Mennonites – they live without personal money or personal possessions and survive because they look after one another from the cradle to the grave. And despite what might seem like poverty to some people, they were the happiest people I've ever met. They read no newspapers, watch no television and take turns to prepare the meals for the whole community to share.

They wear their Christian beliefs lightly even though some are really serious, such as their absolute belief in pacifism and a life of non-violence. During the Nazi persecutions of WWII, many of them fled from Germany and settled in Pennsylvania. One of their earliest supporters was Dietrich Bonhoeffer who preached passive resistance against Adolph Hitler and was executed.

These people influenced me like no other I have met, and their happiness with their life of poverty reminded me of my own farm labourers' family during WWII. They shun material wealth that so many pursue these days and have new communities opening all over the world by people who realise the modern way of the world is not bringing happiness.

# 16. Sunday Assembly

*Church Service or Pop Concert?*

I was concerned about attending this service because it was for young people and was more like a pop concert than a church service.

Sunday Assembly is a non-religious gathering founded by Sanderson Jones and Pippa Evans in 2013. The gatherings are for non-religious people who want a similar experience to a church service, but do not have Christian beliefs or a belief in God. As of 2019, assemblies are established in 48 locations

around the world with the majority in Europe and the United States. They are run and funded by volunteers, and the one I attended was in London.

Stand-up comedians Sanderson Jones and Pippa Evans both wanted something like church but without God. The first event, attended by over 300 people, was held in a deconsecrated church in Islington, London, but due to the limited size of this building, later meetings have been held in the Conway Hall. Since then, events have continued to be held twice a month, with some attracting as many as 600 people.

Sunday Assembly generated much press interest and has been covered on television on the BBC's The Late Show. In 2013, it started an Indiegogo campaign which raised £33,668 to fund a digital platform to help grow the organisation. The formation of satellite congregations was promoted with a 40-day tour through the United Kingdom, Ireland, the USA and Australia. However, some Christians objected to its rejection of God and the idea of an afterlife, and others alleged that raising money is the main goal of the organisation. That said, part of the New York City branch split off because they wanted to emphasise the atheist element more than the founders did. Sunday Assembly has been the subject of widespread academic research, and a six-month longitudinal study of participants has shown a statistically significant

improvement in participants' wellbeing. Following the initial events held in London, Sunday Assemblies have been held in about 90 cities around the world. Since 2018, Sunday Assembly has moved away from its original centralised model. Attendees listen to talks given by celebrity speakers and sing songs by artists such as Stevie Wonder. Some run social clubs and community support events. From my own point of view, I felt it was nothing like a church service and if what I wanted was a pop concert, I'd rather go to the real thing.

# The Author

Brian Boughton graduated in Medicine and Surgery, and was later awarded a postgraduate research degree.

He cared for patients with serious blood diseases, taught medical students and young doctors, and carried out research. During his clinical and research training, he became a Fellow of the Royal College of Physicians and the Royal College of Pathologists, and was elected to the Royal Society of Medicine and the American Association for the Advancement of Science. He served on the editorial boards of international scientific journals, and in 1978 delivered the Plenary Lecture of the British Society of Haematology in Oxford. He worked in university hospitals in Oxford, Birmingham and Southampton, in Queens University in Canada, and the Scripps Research Institute in California. He performed some of the first bone marrow and stem cell transplants in the United Kingdom, and carried out the world's first trial of cancer immunotherapy. He led a research team which published 250 scientific papers and produced ten MSc and PhD graduates. He lectured all over the world, eventually finishing his medical

career as a professor in the University of Southern California. In retirement in the UK, he and his wife renovated a Georgian villa, kept honey bees, manufactured champagne cider and became ocean sailors. Having left medicine, he became a newspaper editor and entered UK party politics. He has published eight other books.

## PUBLISHED BY THE AUTHOR

Pig's Paradise

The Cynics Vade Mecum

England's Lost Pilgrim Trail

Long Live the King

Bananarama

Saturnalia

The Cynics Vade Mecum (2nd Edition)

Greasy Poles and Glass Ceilings